Understand Your Child's Development

For the Muslim Parent

DJARABI KITABS PUBLISHING

Dallas, Texas

AUTHORS

Jameela Ho

Irna Fathurrubayah

Weronika Ozpolat

Nabila Ikram

Afshan Mohammed

Hannah Morris

Understand Your Child's Development

Copyright © 2019 by Jameela Ho, Irna Fathurrubayah, Weronica Ozpolat, Nabila Ikram, Afshan Mohammed, Hannah Morris for each's respective chapter. All rights reserved.

All rights reserved. Printed in the United States of America. No part of this book may be used or reproduced in any manner whatsoever without written permission except in the case of brief quotations embodied in critical articles or reviews.

For information contact:

DJARABI KITABS PUBLISHING

PO BOX 703733

DALLAS, TX 75370

www.djarabikitabs.com

Cover design by Sam Rog

ISBN-10: 1-947148-28-1

ISBN-13: 978-1-947148-28-4

EPUB ISBN-10: 1-947148-29-X

EPUB ISBN-13: 978-1-947148-29-1

Library of Congress Control Number: 2019943647

First Edition: June 2019

10 9 8 7 6 5 4 3 2 1

DEDICATION

To all Muslim parents who are striving to be the best parent they can be.

CONTENTS

CHAPTER 1 Developing Thinking Skills 1

CHAPTER 2 Facilitating Intelligence 22

CHAPTER 3 Supporting Speech & Language Development 40

CHAPTER 4 Promoting Motor Skills..62

CHAPTER 5 Nurturing Healthy Physical Growth 75

CHAPTER 6 Fostering Emotional Development 87

CHAPTER 7 Cultivating Morality..101

ABOUT THE AUTHORS 116

AUTHORS' NOTES

Thank you to all the expert authors who have contributed to make this book a reality.

Thank you to all the children, whom we have taught or interacted with, who gave us the experience that we could pass on.

Chapter One
Developing Thinking Skills
Jameela Ho

In the field of education and child development there are two names that are associated with the development of thinking skills: Piaget and Vygotsky. Piaget's theory is based on the observation that children learn to think about the world around them through their own actions. Vygostsky's theory is based on how children learn to think during their social interactions with others.

PIAGET COGNITIVE DEVELOPMENTAL THEORY

This theory says that children's thinking develops in stages: the sensorimotor stage; the preoperational stage; the concrete operational stage; and the formal operational stage. It assumes that all children go through these stages in this order but the rate at which each child goes through them is affected by the child's genetics and environment. What this means is that parents can play an important role in providing an enriching environment and varied experiences.

You will see how in the following sections.

1. The Sensorimotor Stage (0 to 2 Years)

A newborn first uses reflexes to make movements such as sucking or grasping. By one month, he learns new movements by repeating actions that he has made by chance, such as thumb sucking. In these early stages, your baby's focus is on his own bodily movements.

From 4 months to 8 months, your baby starts to notice his actions on his surroundings so he will repeat his actions to produce the effect it has on his environment. For example, he may kick his legs to make a mobile move.

At about 8 months to 12 months, your baby can coordinate body movements to problem solve and reach a goal. He can push away something in order to grasp an object such as pushing away a cushion to grasp a toy. Your baby can anticipate events, such as predicting that you will be leaving when you put on your *hijab*, as well as imitate new behaviours that he doesn't normally do.

From 12 months to 18 months, your toddler can repeat behaviours with slight variations to reach his goals. In other words, he can problem solve by exploring different actions until a goal is reached. He is also better at imitating the actions of others and using these actions in his problem solving. For example, your toddler can fit a shape into a hole by turning the shape different ways.

At 18 months to 24 months, your toddler is able to make mental representations. This means that he can think about the solution to a problem in his head without having to perform an action first. He will also be able to recall a behaviour of a model who is not present and copy it at a later time.

<u>What You Can Do</u>

As you can see, your baby needs to move to learn about his actions. This means that you should limit swaddling to sleep or nap time and not during active, alert times. From 4 months, you can provide your baby with mobiles above his crib or pram and even ones that come with a mat for lying on the floor.

Since your baby at 8 months can anticipate behaviour, you can start playing games such as peek-a-boo and round-and-round-the-garden. In peek-a-boo, your baby will anticipate the moment you will appear behind your hands, while in round-and-round-the-garden he will anticipate the moment your fingers will walk up his arm or leg and tickle him under the arm (see Activity section on how to play this game.)

From 12 months, you can provide your toddler with activities such as stacking blocks, crayons and paper and shape sorting games. First, you can model how to use each one so your toddler can imitate your actions and then he can try to do them himself.

Why Modelling Good Behaviour Is Important For Your Child

From birth to one month, your baby can mimic your facial expressions and gestures. However, it is not until he can move and control his limbs, from about 4 months to 8 months, that he can copy actions on objects. By the time your toddler is 18 months, he can imitate the behavior of others and can even infer their intentions and perspectives from observing what they do. At 2 years of age, your child will be able to imitate many everyday behaviours of people who play an important role in his life, such as mummy and daddy.

So from birth to 2 years, your child is already observing you and learning about how to behave. The behaviour that you want your child to have should be the behaviour that he sees from you. If you want him to have good behaviour then you should model this kind of behaviour for him.

This is why it is so important for you to always be aware of your own behaviour and try to improve upon it. No one is perfect but if you're constantly mindful of how you behave then you can try to act differently.

2. The Preoperational Stage (2 to 7 years)

During this period, children increasingly use mental representations. This means that they're thinking more in their heads. With this ability comes your child's imaginative or make believe play.

As your child moves from 2 years to 7 years of age, his play becomes more complex. Instead of using a physical object to represent something, your child will use his imagination. For example, he will begin by using a cup to play pretend drinking. Then, in lieu of a cup, he will use a block and, some time later, he will pretend to drink without holding any object.

The play also becomes more complex in terms of the type of actions the players use, the roles that a child takes on and the story lines that are being played out with peers and friends. Compare this play of two 3 year olds below with the play of 5-year-olds after that.

"I have ice-cream," Fatimah informs no one in particular as she picks up a round flat construction piece and connects it to a stick piece.

She glances at Aliyah and picks another round flat piece and a stick piece to make one more.
"Here," she announces as she gives it to Aliyah. Aliyah takes it, looks at it, then makes one herself.
"Ice-cream!" Aliyah declares.

Compare that with these 5 year olds in their sociodramatic play:

"I'm the mum," Khadijah declares. "I'm going to cook some food."

"I'm the child," Amina says as she sits down at the table in the kitchen play area. "Mummy I'm hungry!"

"Food is coming," Khadijah replies, as she stirs a pot and stacks some plastic food onto plates.

Farah enters the kitchen play area and asks, "Can I play?"

As Khadiajh places the plates on the table in front of Amina, she tells Farah, "You're the baby. Come here baby. It's time to eat."

Even though Fatimah and Aliyah can pretend the puzzle pieces are ice cream, their actions are to make the ice creams by holding it. There are no roles or story to their play whereas the three older girls create a complete story line with roles for each that requires many different actions.

<u>Why Play is Important for Your Child</u>

In the 3-year-olds example above, Fatimah is using cognitive skills to mentally transform the construction pieces into an ice-cream. She is using language to communicate with another child, and she is using social skills to start a play episode with her. Her motor skills are demonstrated by the picking up of the construction pieces and connecting them using the fine muscles in her fingers and thumb and her hand and eye coordination. It involves a whole range of skills from cognition and language to social and motor skills.

In the 5-year-olds' play, they are learning about social roles, perspective taking, turn-taking and cooperation as well as all the other cognitive, language and motor skills.

<u>Children's Cognitive Play Can Be Seen in Three Stages:</u>

1. Functional Play (Birth to 2 years)

Children's play at this stage is characterised by the use of their senses (touch, taste, hearing, sight and smell) and motor movements (body, arms etc.). Which is why it is also referred to as sensorimotor play or practice play. Infants are basically practising the use of their senses and motors.

2. Symbolic Play (2 to 6 years)

At these ages, children begin to use symbolic thought to transform an object or themselves into something else.

a) Constructive Play. Children use objects to represent other objects. As in the above example, Fatimah uses the construction pieces to represent ice-cream. Another example is the use of building blocks to represent a tower. This is where children build things and make them represent something. Read the **"Benefits of Constructive Play"** on my blog.

b) Dramatic and Sociodramatic Play. Children use imaginary roles in play. In dramatic play, the child plays by him/herself while pretending to be someone else, whereas sociodramatic play involves a group of children who take on roles and coordinate their play.

3. Games with Rules Play (6 to 8 years)

School age children's thinking is more developed and they can, therefore, follow rules. Their play will be characterised by games that have a set of rules. This includes indoor play with board games and computer games and outdoor play with sports or children's games such as 'tips.'

Through play, children are exploring the world and developing skills that will help them to live in the world. Notice in functional play that children use their senses and motors to explore their immediate environment and to practice using these skills. In symbolic play they are using their minds to explore the world; with its objects and its people.

Children who often engage in sociodramatic play are better at social skills, sustained attention, memory, logical reasoning, language, literacy, imagination and perspective taking.

13 | Understand Your Child's Development

Age	Stage	What Your Child Can Do
0-2 years	Functional Play	• Use the 5 senses and body movements to explore and play
2-6 years	Symbolic Play	• Use symbolic thought to transform an object or themselves • Constructive play – use objects to represent other objects • Dramatic and Sociodramatic play – use imaginary roles to play
6-8 years	Games with Rules Play	• Can follow rules

Table 1.1 Children's Stages of Play

<u>What You Can Do</u>

It is important that you provide your child with the appropriate environment to encourage his play. This includes not only providing the appropriate materials but also providing the support.

Appropriate support means knowing at roughly what stage your child is at and preparing the environment. For example, if your child is at the dramatic play stage then there is no point in getting him to play soccer. The best that you can get him to do is to kick the ball; never mind following the rules! If you've ever watched 5-year-olds playing a game of soccer, then you'll see that the only rule they have is to kick the ball into the goal. There are no player positions, all 22 children will chase the ball across the field and try to kick it. Likewise, if you have a 1-year-old child then do not buy her that expensive toy house. The best that she can do with it is to bang it on something, throw it, suck it or chew it!

To help you provide appropriate support for your child's play, here are some suggested play materials for each play stage:

Functional Play: Toys that make noises or movements such as rattles, squeeze balls and activity boards, and toys that can be put together and taken apart such as stacking cups, bucket with shapes.

Symbolic Play: Construction toys such as blocks, lego, connector toys, clay and play dough, and almost anything that children can construct with. For dramatic play, provide props such as telephones, assorted uniforms/clothing, doctor's kit, and miniature toys such as cars, houses and cooking utensils.

Games with Rules Play: Board games, card games, group games such as chasing and sports.

The other thing that you can do for your child is to play with him. Children love to play so if you can spend 10 minutes each day to do something that your child loves to do then you'll form a deeper connection with your child. This is called Special Play Time. You can read more about it on my blog in the article **"Connect With Your Child During Special Time."** When you play, you let your child lead and decide on what to do. You are the playmate that's willing to follow your child's lead. Don't ever takeover.

Prophet Muhammad ﷺ would also play with his grandchildren. In this *hadith*, he was "chasing" his grandson, and it shows how important it is that you play with your child too. Ya'la Ibn Mura says, "I went out with the Prophet ﷺ for a food invitation. Al-Hussain, son of Ali, was playing in the street, whereupon the Prophet ﷺ hurried towards him, in front of the people, to catch him while Al-Hussain ran right and left to escape. Moreover, he used to take Osama Ibn Zaid and Al-Hassan Ibn Ali and place them on his thighs. Then, he would tightly hug them and say, "O Allah have mercy on them as I have mercy on them." (Al-Bukhari, 6003)

3. The Concrete Operational Stage (7 to 11 Years)

Children's thinking becomes more organised and logical during this stage but their thinking is based on concrete information. They cannot yet think abstractly. Everything needs to be seen and perceived. During this stage, children need to have many experiences with concrete objects. Your child will need to be able to manipulate them.

<u>Why Hands-on Learning Experiences Are Important For Your Child</u>

When children learn, they need to have many hands-on experiences. This means that they need to be able to see, smell, touch, hear and possibly taste what they are learning about. Give them lots of experiences in this before they can move into abstract thinking.

Concrete experiences provide the background knowledge to help your child make connections to build new knowledge. If I say cow, your child would probably think of mooing, milk, brown cow or black and white ones, four legs, beef, burgers and maybe even that it is a farm animal. This is his background knowledge that he probably got from watching television or reading books.

The more experiences your child has with the subject, the more background he can bring to it. Sometimes, passively reading or watching television is not enough. If your child has ever been to a cattle farm, he will probably remember the smell of manure or the action of milking a cow. He could also tell how big they are and remember the feel of their skin. These are the concrete experiences that he can bring to learn more about the subject. Without any background knowledge, the word cow will have no meaning.

Don't limit your child's reading to only fiction books. Although reading is passive, it will still provide him with background knowledge. Children have a fascination with the world around them, from how things work to why things are the way they are. Nurture this fascination to ask questions and seek more knowledge and experiences.

What You Can Do

Here are some things that you can do to help your child in the concrete operational stage

1. Use the five senses to teach.

2. Go on excursions and field trips. Give your child lots of diverse experiences.

3. Make good use of manipulatives and objects that can be handled.

4. Read non-fiction as well as fiction books.

4. The Formal Operational Stage (11+ Years)

Your adolescent can now think in abstract and logical thoughts by internally reflecting on thoughts and ideas. There are two types of thinking that he does. The first is deductive reasoning where, when faced with a problem, he will begin with a general theory to the problem and then deduce from what might happen and come up with a specific prediction.

The second type of thinking is propositional thought where he can evaluate the logic of a person's statement without referring to real-world situations. This requires language to be able to reason it out verbally.

These two types of thinking are the reason why your teenager will start arguing with you. He starts to think logically and to him, your requests or demands may seem illogical and unreasonable. He will point out to you the illogic of what you have just said and he will debate on why his view is the most logical. He will question your reasons and to him "Because I said so" does not make any sense.

What You Can Do

Along this path of questioning everything, he will start to think about justice, freedom, poverty and religion. If you haven't given your child a solid foundation in Islam then he will question the validity of his acts of worship. Be ready with the reasons behind Islamic concepts and acts. Know your Islam. Teach him the reasons.

As for questioning you, as long as your teenager can see the logic behind your requests and understand the reasons then he will do as you say. He needs to clean his room because Muslims are clean. He needs to do the household chores because families are made of people who share the workload and work together. He needs to study so that he can get good marks so he can have choices as to what he would like to do. He needs to work so that he can support his own family when he marries. He needs to do good deeds so he can get to *jannah*.

If your teenager starts to argue with you then let him have his say. Quote this *hadith*, be the role model and stop arguing. Prophet Muhammad ﷺ said, "Whoever does not argue when he is in the wrong will have a home built for him on the edge of Paradise. Whoever avoids it when he in the right will have a home built for him in the middle of Paradise. And whoever improves his own character, a home will be built for him in the highest part of Paradise." (Sunan Abu Dawud, 4800)

Age	Stage	What your child can do
0-2 years	Sensorimotor	• Newborns use reflexes • 4-8 months – repeat an action • 8-12 months – coordinate body movements to problem solve • 12-18 months – explore different actions to problem solve • 18-24 months – make mental representations (think about the solution to a problem)
2-7 years	Preoperational	• Increased mental representations • Play imaginatively (see Table 1)
7-11 years	Concrete Operational	• Thinking based on concrete information • Cannot yet think abstractly
11+ years	Formal Operational	• Thinking is abstract and logical • Use deductive reasoning • Use propositional thought

Table 1.2 Piaget Cognitive Development

That was Piaget's comprehensive Cognitive Developmental Theory. We will now leave it and briefly turn to Vygostsky's Sociocultural Theory.

VYGOTSKY SOCIOCULTURAL THEORY

Vygotsky believed that children learn through interacting with others. One way is through the Zone of Proximal Development.

The Zone of Proximal Development

The Zone of Proximal Development (ZPD) is the difference between what the learner can do by himself and what he can do with help. This is the area that teachers, parents, tutors, siblings and others work in when they help someone to learn.

If left by themselves, children will only do what they know. They will not be able to go beyond this point. So to get them onto the next level they need help by interacting with someone more knowledgeable. This is where you, the parent, comes in. You quickly assess what your child can do and you plan lessons and learning activities that build on what he knows.

If you teach your child something he already knows then you are not teaching him in the ZPD but you are reteaching him something he can already do. This is very demotivating and he will quickly become bored or disruptive.

If you start teaching your child above the ZPD, at what he cannot yet do, he will become confused and demotivated as well as disruptive. You are teaching at too high a level. In this case, you would need to back up a few steps until you find what your child can do and start teaching the next step from there.

Take the example of learning to walk. You cannot teach your baby to run if he cannot yet walk and you cannot teach him to walk if he cannot yet stand. If what your baby can do is crawl then his ZPD is to stand with support once his legs are strong enough. Once he can stand with support then the next step is to stand without support before you start to hold his hands and 'walk' him.

<u>What You Can Do</u>

Prophet Muhammad ﷺ always taught his Companions within their ZPD. What is the proof of this? He gave different teachings to different Companions. He knew where they were at, Islamically, and what each needed to learn and do next to improve themselves.

Abu Huraira reported, "A man came to the Prophet ﷺ and he said, 'Advise me.' The Prophet ﷺ said, 'Do not be angry.' The man repeated his request and the Prophet ﷺ said, 'Do not be angry.' " (Al Bukhari, 5765)

Abu Huraira narrated, "My friend (the Prophet ﷺ) advised me to do three things and I shall not leave them till I die. They are: to fast three days every month, to offer the *duha* prayer, and to offer *witr* before sleeping. (Al Bukhari, 1124,1180)

With your own child, ask yourself what you know he knows or can do or conduct a quick assessment. Then find out what the next step on that learning continuum is that he cannot yet do or know. This is his ZPD. Once you have found his ZPD, plan the lessons that will guide him through this level until he has mastered it before moving onto the next step on the learning continuum. Make sure to have as much hands on activities as possible and ask questions that generate thinking.

ACTIVITIES FOR COGNITIVE DEVELOPMENT

1. For Babies

Play tickling games. How to play round-and-round-the-garden: Take your baby's hand and gently draw circles in his palm while saying, "Round and round the garden like a teddy bear." Next, walk your fingers up his arm as you say, "One step, two step." Finally, tickle him gently under his arm as you say, "Tickle you under there!"

2. For Dramatic Play

Set out some playdough on the table. To encourage pretend play, include some props. For a cooking theme, include cooking toys such as spoons, plate, cup, pan. For a farm or animal theme, include mini farm animals or jungle animals. For role play, include different types of lego people such as firemen, astronauts and so on.

3. For Concrete Experiences in Conservation of Liquids

Set up different types of containers, some with the same capacity but different shapes. Give children a jug of water to experiment by filling the containers and comparing the amounts. Arrange in order going from the one that holds the least to the most.

4. For Your Adolescent's Logic

Have your teenager prepare a 10-minute family talk on an Islamic topic such as "Why everyone needs to pay *zakat*" or "The benefits of praying." Have him present it to the family much like a Friday *kutbah*.

5. For teaching in the ZPD

What is your child struggling with? Write down where your child is at with his struggles. What can he do? Search that topic and find the learning continuum. Identify where your child is on the learning continuum and teach the next step.

Chapter Two
Facilitating Intelligence
Irna Fathurrubayah

One of the biggest blessings that Allah ﷻ has bestowed upon us as human beings is intelligence. It is a quality which makes us different from any other of Allah's creations. As stated by Utz (2011), while modern psychology suggests that intelligence solely revolves around worldly accomplishment, *al'aql* or intelligence in Islam essentially emphasizes "spiritual understanding" in order to achieve our utmost goal, the hereafter (p.170). Intelligence should be the tool for us to succeed not only in this dunya, but also in the *akhirah*. Allah ﷻ the Exalted says in the Quran:

"...And the home of the Hereafter is best for those who fear Allah ﷻ; then will you not reason?" (Quran 12:109)

Intelligence or smartness has been one of the qualities that every parent wants their kids to have. But what is smartness? Is it all about getting the highest score in the IQ test or getting the "A" grade in school subjects? What about the kids who are not well-accomplished in those tests? Are they smart enough or are they less of a genius? You will discover the answers in this chapter.

GARDNER'S MULTIPLE INTELLIGENCES

Smartness had been widely known to be solely associated with the Intelligence Quotient (IQ). According to Utz (2011), mathematical and verbal are the main aptitudes which the IQ assesses (p.169). Yet, this limited number of aptitudes defines whether an individual is a genius, average, or less smart. It was not until an American Developmental psychologist, Howard Gardner, identified eight distinct intelligences and developed the theory of Multiple Intelligences that the smartness paradigm changed, especially in the field of education. This theory celebrates every innate talent that every child has been blessed with, because now smartness is seen as more than about scoring well in standardized tests.

So, what is Gardner's Multiple Intelligences? The concept that Gardner's theory has brought is that we are all endowed with at least eight different types of intelligences rather than a single ability. Connell (2005) explains that each of the intelligences has a particular area in our brain which can be either well, moderately or less developed (p.66) and according to Armstrong (2009) these intelligences can be developed through particular treatments (p.15). Below is a brief description about each of the eight types which may help parents to identify their child's multiple intelligences.

1. Logical Mathematical

Due to their immense ability in using logical thinking and numbers in various ways, the child whose logical mathematical intelligence is highly developed is described as number smart. This child's strength is in reasoning, computing, analyzing, and research. A number smart child tends to love computer programming, chess, science experiments, logical brainteasers, and Math puzzles. Learning with diagrams, numerical data, table and timelines have tremendous appeal. Encourage your number smart child to develop in the area of astronomy, science, mathematics, or computer programming.

2. Spatial

The child with well-developed spatial intelligence has a remarkable ability in visualizing things inside the head and manifest it into two or three-dimensional creative arts. In other words, this child is picture smart as pictures are easily created in the mind. The picture smart child is excellent at drawing, geometry, designing, mapping, crafting and decorating and enjoys creating two or three dimensional art. The best way to approach a picture smart learner is through mind-mapping, graphics, and other visual presentations. For the picture smart child the field of architecture, graphic designing, interior and visual arts may be most suitable.

3. Verbal-linguistic

The child who has strength in verbal-linguistic intelligence excels in using words in variety of ways which encompasses reading, speaking and writing. This word smart child prefers to learn through reading, note taking, oral presentation, storytelling, and lectures. Poems, word-puzzles, debates, story-writing, and journaling tend to draw this child's interest. This innate talent which can be nurtured can possibly lead to a career in writing, speaking, teaching, journalism, or law in the future.

3. Bodily-Kinesthetic

The child with a highly-developed bodily-kinesthetic intelligence is described as body smart. There is tremendous ability in a wide range of physical skills. The body is used adroitly, including in hands-on activities. The body smart child learns best when engaged in touching and moving. Various kinds of sport, outdoor games, role-playing and practical experiments are activities the body smart child would love to be involved in. Some of the preferred careers of people with this type of intelligence are sports coach, professional athlete, halal food chef, surgeon and physiotherapist.

5. Interpersonal

The term for this type of intelligence is people smart. Having strong interpersonal intelligence gives your child a distinctive quality in the ability to deal with peers and people. This child is excellent at understanding people, is an eloquent communicator and a natural leader. The people smart child easily blends in with others, often enjoying social activities, team games and discussions. The best way to approach people smart learners is through team projects and group discussion. Leadership, politics, humanitarian, marketing, coaching and mentoring are the preferred areas of people with strong interpersonal intelligence.

6. Musical

The term for the child with strength in this type of intelligence is music smart or we can say sound smart. A sound smart child has exquisite ability to perceive and produce rhythm and tones. This child may be good at singing rhymes or even creating ones, reciting Quran beautifully with perfect *tajweed*, or mimicking other's voices or sounds. He or she enjoys listening and reciting various kinds of rhythmic and melodious tones. Using rhymes in lessons will make the sound smart child learn better. Your sound smart child may be the next international Qari like Mishary Rashid Alafasy or may be the next inspirational *nasheed* singer like Zain Bikha.

7. Intrapersonal

The child who has highly developed intrapersonal intelligence is very reflective and metacognitive and is naturally introverted and intuitive. He or she has a strong inner wisdom to understand the self (thoughts, feelings, values, and goals.) Having strength in this type of intelligence is described as self-smart. Journaling, writing, reading inspirational books, making scrapbooks, enjoying nature, creating to-do-lists are kinds of activities that interests the self-smart child most. This child is a self-directed and independent learner and so enjoys a quiet environment to study at his or her own pace. Give plenty of opportunity for this child to set own goals. Your little self-smart child may become a future inspiring author, psychologist, Islamic counselor or halal entrepreneur.

8. Naturalistic

Nature smart is best used to describe the child who is gifted with an excellent ability in identifying and classifying living beings and having a deep understanding about its relationships. This is the child who has well-developed naturalistic intelligence. This child is a natural-born environmentalist. The topic of global warming and pollution may interest him or her most. The nature smart child will enjoy walking through a nature trail, listening to the sounds of birds and waterfalls, sowing and growing various seeds, doing science experiments and observing microscopic organisms. Engaging your nature smart child with the natural environment is the best way to help him or her to learn at their best. Environmental jobs (activist, engineer, or scientist,) herbalist, veterinarian, and zoologist are some kind of the careers that allow nature-smart people to make the most of their excellent ability.

Intelligence	What your child can do
Logical Mathematical (Number Smart)	• Precisely solves mathematical problem and logical puzzles • Interprets numerical data and diagrams accurately
Spatial (Picture Smart)	• Figures geometric objects and directions out accurately • Creates two or three-dimensional object precisely from his or her vivid imagination
Verbal-linguistic (Word Smart)	• Expresses his or her ideas through words effectively • Produces eloquent speeches and/or written pieces
Bodily-Kinesthetic (Body Smart)	• Moves his or her body adroitly • Precisely uses his or her hands to create or repair things • Expresses his or her ideas through gestures accurately
Interpersonal (People Smart)	• Communicates eloquently and effectively • Gets along very well with anyone

	• Being a leader among the group of his or her peers
Musical (Sound Smart)	• Identifies sounds and tones sensitively • Produces *in-tune* voices • Creates harmonious rhythmic sounds
Intrapersonal (Self Smart)	• Understands his or her own strengths and weaknesses • Plans and sets goals for him or herself • Self-study
Naturalistic (Nature Smart)	• Identifies living beings • Classifies plants and animals • Understands causes and effects of environmental issues

Table 2.1 Multiple Intelligences

WHY IT'S IMPORTANT TO KNOW YOUR CHILD'S INTELLIGENCE

By identifying the type of intelligence your child has, you can use this strength to help with learning and accelerate this innate talent. In this way, your child's gift from Allah will not remain unexplored and wasted but instead, your child can add valuable contributions to the Muslim *ummah*.

Looking back over the Islamic History, it is amazing to know about how the Prophet ﷺ's companions, and the Muslims afterwards in the medieval age, had excelled in their specific areas. This era is well-known as the golden age of Islamic civilization. Valuable inventions and scientific ideas in astronomy, architecture, engineering, mathematics, medicine, philosophy, arts, agriculture, language and literature flourished in this era.

It was Al-Jahiz, a Muslim philosopher from Iraq who had incredible verbal-linguistic and intrapersonal intelligence in the 8th century. He wrote around two hundred books on many topics. While in the mathematics field there was a notable number smart Muslim scholar in the 10th century. He was Al-Khawarizmi, the father of algebra. His ideas have given a valuable contribution to the advanced development of mathematics. Another excellent number smart Muslim scholar in medieval times was al-Batani, an astronomer as well as a mathematician, who discovered the fundamental concept of trigonometry. Among the numerous great Muslim scholars of the *ummah*, several have given huge contributions to the world because of their innate talents.

Besides, let's contemplate for a minute. Who was blessed with and shone with an exceptional interpersonal intelligence in the history of mankind? No doubt, we must look up to our foremost exemplary figure, the Prophet Muhammad ﷺ. He treated and dealt with everyone in a perfect manner. As a result, he was beloved to them and he successfully invited those who went against him into Islam. By following the manner of the Prophet ﷺ we use this intelligence as means to please Allah ﷻ. The Prophet ﷺ said, "Verily the best of you are those who are best in attitude." (Al-Bukhari, 3366)

So it goes for the use of rhythmic intelligence. It may bring huge rewards for us. Not through music, but rhythmic intelligence can be how well someone recites the Quran beautifully with perfect *tajweed*. Some of excellent sound smart figures in this era are Muhammad Al-Muqit and Sheikh Mansour Al-Salimi. Besides having amazing Quran recitation, they are prominent in performing *nasheeds* and Islamic poems as well.

OBSERVE YOUR CHILD FOR SIGNS OF MULTIPLE INTELLIGENCE

How do you know which intelligence your child has? The simple answer is through observations. Watch your child and notice how he or she likes to learn. Or, if you see your child struggling in an area, make a note that this area of intelligence is not his or her natural preferred intelligence.

Let me give you two examples of how observations can reveal a child's natural intelligence by relating my classroom observations.

At the beginning of the first school year, I initially noticed a student with a strong verbal-linguistic intelligence among my 6th grade students after I had given a number of writing assignments. She narrated a long sequence of harmonious paragraphs whereas the majority of my students just simply wrote several short sentences. I gradually noticed that her excellent ability to narrate and sequence words was not only found in reading assignments but also the way she verbally answered questions in various subjects.

Another example happened a few years back when I assisted an elementary school teacher in teaching 1st grade. The school was still using conventional teaching where the teachers would simply write sentences on the chalkboard to read aloud together or explain later on, while students would copy it down in their notebook. No illustrations, simply words. There were some students who couldn't keep up with the lessons and made no progress in their reading. I approached each one personally and tried to introduce each word with an illustration that I drew together with them. The children seemed more interested and could understand the lessons I gave. This made me think that how can we expect a picture smart child to learn well through word only lessons? Picture smart children learn their best through images, of course.

If you do not have a clue as to what intelligence your child has then start now and watch him or her closely and take notes. Once you have figured out what intelligence your child has then you can nurture it through activities that enhance that intelligence.

HALAL AND FUN ACTIVITIES FOR YOUR CHILD'S MULTIPLE INTELLIGENCE

Multiple intelligences can flourish if they are well-nurtured. However, as a Muslim, nurturing these intelligences should be within the boundary of Islamic guidance with the hope that they will not only attain worldly achievement but also, ultimately, success in the Hereafter.

These are *halal*, yet fun, activities which you can try to develop and enhance your child's natural intelligence. These eight intelligences can be strengthened through particular activities for each. Let's explore each of them and get your child excited for learning!

There are plenty of ideas for activities that you can do to boost your child's multiple intelligence. These activities are just a few suggestions that hopefully will bring benefits for your child's cognitive development as well as instilling Islamic values.

1. Thematic Bedtime Storytelling

The great benefits of bedtime storytelling are well-known. Bedtime storytelling can promote parent-child bonding, build their imagination, strengthen their memory, improve their sleeping and amazingly work on their cognitive development, especially in linguistic ability. According to Hale et al. (2011), maintaining "language-based bedtime routines" — which includes storytelling —

every night, may bring a long-term positive impact in their cognitive development (verbal skills) as well as their sleep duration.

This thematic bedtime storytelling aims to not only bring a handful of benefits that have been described above, but also to develop your child's knowledge of Islam and the noble characteristics of a Muslim. You can begin this activity by selecting a theme. The themes may include story of the Prophets, which may take 1-2 weeks, in which each Prophet's story may be divided into several days (the bedtime stories should ideally be less than 10 minutes long.) After choosing a theme, parents can list a daily story for each theme. There are various Muslim story books for children available, with stunning illustrations, which you can simply use.

When you read a story try to use language that can easily be understood according to your child's age. To make it more exciting, you can add sound effects such as the sound of a strong wind or the foot-steps of a horse. Sometimes, your child's curious mind may surprise you, so be ready for the question that may pop out all of sudden. Besides, you might want to ask questions to encourage thinking such as how your child thinks the character is feeling and what might possibly happen next in the story. You need to choose the right moments to ask because but you don't want you child to feel as if he or she is being examined for listening.

To further encourage your child's verbal-linguistic intelligence – as this intelligence includes reading, writing and speaking – you can try building a home reading-corner, enrolling your child into foreign language courses, poetry writing, journaling, story writing and library visits. These are just some ideas to get your child started.

2. Home Gardening

Gardening is an interesting activity that you can do with your child. It has numerous profound benefits for both the parent and child. In an article published by **Children Youth and Environmental Center for Research and Design**, from the University of Colorado, it stated that, "...in a qualitative assessment of an intergenerational gardening project, students expressed an increased understanding of ecology, interconnections in nature, and responsibility to care for the environment..." (Mayer-Smith, Bartosh & Peterat, 2007). Gardening requires your child to be closely engaged with nature so it can be a way to enhance the naturalistic intelligence.

Before you start gardening, you may introduce the plants and animals that are mentioned in the Quran and *ahadith* to your child. Choose the easiest plants to grow such as basil (55:12,) ginger (76:17) and fig (95:1.) During this activity you can teach your child the Quranic verses regarding the living creatures that live in that garden such as the bee (16: 68-69,) ants (27:18,) spider (29:41,) worm (34:14) as well as some *ahadith* about the benefits of certain plants, vegetables, or fruits that you are trying to grow.

Other fun activities for the nature smart child may include homesteading, nature photography, nature hiking, herbalism, natural remedies, recycling and waste management.

3. Swimming, Archery and Horseback Riding

You can help to strengthen your child's bodily-kinesthetic intelligence by doing various types of sports. Swimming, horse riding and archery are the kind of sports which are encouraged by the Prophet ﷺ.

These three sports carry tremendous benefits for your child. Professor Robyn Jorgensen from Griffith University stated that children who swim from an early age are more advanced in their language, cognitive and physical development than those who do not. Horseback riding, besides carrying physical benefits, has cognitive benefit as well. A research study, published in **Frontiers in Public Health** journal found that riding horses improves children's ability in performing behavioral tasks and solving arithmetic problems. Amazing benefits also can be found in archery such as improved coordination, balance, concentration and self confidence.

Before you start your child on swimming, archery or horseback riding lessons, you may want to explain how the Prophet ﷺ and his companions used to practice these sports. Read about these activities and let your child get excited about them. Make sure that the lessons are appropriate for your child's age and he or she is happy to take the lessons. Choose a swimming, archery, or horseback riding school or club that is suitable for your child.

Other exciting activities for the body smart child may include cooking lessons, crafting, recycling, repairing things, cycling, skating, and other sports.

4. Quran Recitations, Nasheeds and Rhymes

Quran recitations, vocal-only *nasheeds* and rhymes are the *halal* way for you to cultivate your child's musical intelligence instead of songs with rich musical instruments.

The countless miracles of the Quran that science has revealed will surely amaze those who ponder upon it. Mohamed Ghilan, a neuroscience PhD holder, in his article **How the Quran Shapes the Brain** describes an excellent characteristic of the Quran. He said, "The verses in the Quran rhyme and change rhythm often." This greatly benefits those who listen to it attentively, with a blissful feeling. He also explains that the activation of the brain area which is responsible for musical sound processing also happens when we are attentively listening to the Quran recitation.

However, your purpose on engaging your child with the Quran should not be centered for the sake of musical intelligence, but the purpose is to instill the love of the Quran from an early age so that he or she will always be firmly attached to the Quran throughout life. It is encouraged to start connecting your child with the Quran recitation even during pregnancy.

To get your child connected to the Quran, you can allocate several minutes of quality time daily to attentively — and silently — listen to Quran together. Play the audio of the Quran and guide your child to point to the verses which are being recited on the *mushaf*, either with a finger or a pen. It can be 10 or 15 minutes in the morning, not for longer as children are not able to focus for longer than this. In addition, play Quran recitations during your child's "silent" activities such as while he or she is busy with drawing. It is important to teach your child to be quiet when there is Quran being recited and you should model attentive listening instead of chatting.

You can use music-free rhymes and *nasheeds* in both Islamic lessons, like the five pillars of Islam, the prophets' names, Asma'ul Khusna, months in Islam and daily *duas*, as well as general lessons like map work, country names, geometric shapes, plants and animals' name, etc.

Other activities to engage your sound smart child are reading poetry, singing nasheeds, creating rhymes and the spoken word.

5. Ramadan and Eid Decorating

Ramadan and Eid decorating are the kind of craft-rich activities that you can do to strengthen your child's visual-spatial intelligence. Richard Rende, PhD, leading child psychologist and researcher, points out in his talk about fostering visual-spatial skills that, visual processing in a child's brain is greatly stimulated when doing crafting. Furthermore, he explains that when children do crafts, the same spatial skills are being used as for activities such as geometry. Besides strengthening their visual-spatial intelligence, Ramadan and Eid decorating will specially contribute to our child's enthusiasm in entering the Holy Month of Ramadan and celebrating the Eids.

Create a Ramadan countdown calendar with your child at least a month before the first day of Ramadan and you can start decorating a week before Ramadan. The activities may include sketching a design, selecting the color theme, shopping and preparing for the materials, making decoration crafts, and finally, decorating!

Awesome activities for the picture smart child can be creating various two or three-dimensional art works.

6. Family Visits and Social Activities

The people smart child has leadership ability that needs to be nurtured. Getting your child to take action in helping people will cultivate a sense of responsibility and empathy which are the essential elements of leadership.

You can encourage your child to give donations or charity to needy people or helping neighbours and relatives even for simple things. Always encourage your child to help others.

It can be helping any of their friends, reminding their friends whenever your child finds them doing wrong, or even picking up poor animals that need help.

Another great activity for the people smart child is family visits. Besides developing and enhancing interpersonal intelligence, a frequent family visit could strengthen family kinship as well as instilling a noble character as a Muslim.

Your people smart child will get excited to meet relatives and play with cousins. The more your child interacts and gets along with people, the more he or she will understand others.

You can start these activities by explaining about the Prophet ﷺ 's excellent attitude and manner towards people through storytelling. Then, plan your time to visit relatives and discuss with your child what kind of gift to bring.

Last but not least, at the end of any family visit or social activity let your child tell you how it felt after meeting relatives and helping others.

Present challenging work such as service projects and sibling team work for repairing or cleaning tasks. Also doing volunteering work at a charity organization such as feeding the homeless or fundraising are other activities for your people smart child.

7. Quran and Hadith Journaling

The self smart child loves to reflect, observe and set goals. So, journaling is the perfect activity. Besides nurturing intrapersonal intelligence, Quran and *hadith* journaling will also benefit both you and your child. It will encourage more love towards the Quran while spending quality time together.

This activity starts with a nice notebook (it should be free from animate illustrations) and colourful stationery. Together you and your child can set a daily or weekly schedule for journaling. Choose the ideal time, it can be in the morning or evening. Then, select a place. Journaling can be done outdoors while enjoying nature, not just indoors.

Keep a *tafseer* book on hand, choose a *surah* or *hadith* that is relevant and easy to understand for your child's age, write down the *surah* or *hadith*, explain the meaning and draw the explanation in pictures. Then, ask your child to reflect on what he or she did before and what he or she will do now that the *surah* or *hadith* has been understood. You or your child can write these reflections in the notebook and decorate the page.

Other types of journaling are gratitude journaling, science journaling and self-journaling. These are a few to get your self smart child started.

8. Allowance and Charity Routine

Developing logical-mathematical intelligence can be done through various activities that include any kind of calculation and measurement as the number smart child loves to calculate and reason.

Teaching and giving your child an appropriate allowance may bring a great deal of benefit besides developing logical-mathematical intelligence. As a Muslim, your child must be instilled with how to spend money wisely, live moderately, avoid extravagance and stinginess, and form charity habits from a young age. In this activity, your child will learn to calculate money for spending as well as for charity. It is a great tool to nurture logical-mathematical intelligence and financial skills as well as Islamic values.

You can start giving your child an allowance. School age, around five or six, is the best time. As our currency may be different, I can say the first amount of your child's allowance can be around the price of a kilogram of apples — for a week — and can be added yearly accordingly. Your child can buy simple things with the allowance, such as story books or stationery. If your child wants something more expensive, like a bicycle, then he or she can save for it. Create a charity jar and a savings jar. At the end of the month, your child can use the money collected in the charity jar to give to charity. For the older child such as the pre-teen, you can start to teach budgeting.

An important thing to remember is not to tie your child's allowance with the chores and tasks that he or she has to do. This is because your child may perceive those tasks as a paid-job rather than his or her own responsibility within the family.

Conclusion

In every activity, each type of intelligence cannot work by itself rather they work together (Amstrong 2009). For instance, when your child is engaging in a decorating activity, he or she will use spatial intelligence to design and pick colours for the ornament, bodily-kinesthetic to cut and fold the paper, logical-mathematical to measure the size of the papers needed as well as verbal-linguistic intelligence to discuss his or her ideas with you.

Besides the halal activities mentioned above, you can try other ideas for halal activities to enhance and develop each of the eight multiple intelligences. Identifying and nurturing intelligence – in a halal way – in your child is important to help him or her learn and excel with their instinctive talent.

References

Yost, B., & Chawla, L. (2009). *Benefits of gardening for children,* Fact Sheet #3, Aug2009. Children, Youth and Environments Center for Research and Design,University of Colorado at Denver and Health Sciences Center. Retrieved April 4, 2018, from http://www.peecworks.org/PEEC/PEEC_Reports/01795CA8-001D0211.32/.

Al-Hassani, S. T., Saoud, R., & Woodcock, E. (2007). *1001 Inventions: Muslim Heritage in Our World* (2nd ed.). Manchester, Great Britain, UK: the Foundation for Science Technology and Civilisation.

Armstrong, T. (2009). *Multiple Intelligences in the Classroom* (3rd ed.). Alexandria, VA: ASCD.

Connell, J. D. (2005). *Brain-based Strategies to Reach Every Learner.* New York: Scholastic.

Dalhat, Y. (2015). The concept of al-aql (reason) in Islam. *International Journal of Humanities and Social Science. Vol.5, No 9 (1).* Retrieved January 31, 2018, from http://www.ijhssnet.com/journals/Vol_5_No_9_1_September_2015/8.pdf

Hale, L., Berger, L. M., LeBourgeois, M. K., & Brooks-Gunn, J. (2011). A Longitudinal Study of Preschoolers' Language-Based Bedtime Routines, Sleep Duration, and Wellbeing. *Journal of Family Psychology : JFP : Journal of the Division of Family Psychology of the American Psychological Association (Division 43)*, *25*(3), 423–433. http://doi.org/10.1037/a0023564

Utz, A. (2011). *Psychology from the Islamic Perspective.* Riyadh, Saudi Arabia: International Islamic Publishing House.

Vaid, Dawood. (September 11, 2015). Multiple intelligence at school (part I). Retrieved January 28, 2018, from **http://blog.islamiconlineuniversity.com/multiple-intelligence-at-school-part-1/**.

George Lucas Educational Foundation. (July 20, 2016). Multiple Intelligences: What Does the Research Say?. Retrieved January 28, 2018, from **https://www.edutopia.org/multiple-intelligences-research**.

Griffith University. (August 13, 2013). *Swimming a smart move for kids*[Press release]. Retrieved April 6, 2018, from **https://www.youtube.com/watch?v=-Pu_ZPQFwP0**

Griffith University. (November 18, 2012). *Study shows kids are smarter if they swim* [Press release]. Retrieved April 6, 2018, from https://www.youtube.com/watch?v=fmh1sOTo4Iw.

Elmer's Let's Bond Fostering Visual Spatial Skills [Advertisement]. (March 20, 2014). Retrieved April 6, 2018, from https://www.youtube.com/watch?v=IuY3JyHIFOU.

Ohtani, N., Kitagawa, K., Mikami, K., Kitawaki, K., Akiyama, J., Fuchikami, M., ... Ohta, M. (2017). Horseback Riding Improves the Ability to Cause the Appropriate Action (Go Reaction) and the Appropriate Self-control (No-Go Reaction) in Children. *Frontiers in Public Health*, 5, 8. http://doi.org/10.3389/fpubh.2017.00008.

Ghilan, M. (2012). How the Quran shapes the brain. Retrieved April 5, 2018, from http://www.islamicity.org/5657/how-the-quran-shapes-the-brain/.

Farooqi, S. (March 27, 2017). How to Teach Children the Qur'an. Retrieved April 3, 2018, from https://sadaffarooqi.com/2017/03/27/how-to-teach-children-the-quran/.

A. (March 3, 2015). 10 Reasons to Teach Your Kids Archery. Retrieved April 6, 2018, from https://www.archery360.com/2015/03/03/10-reasons-to-teach-your-kids-archery/.

Lack, E. (April, 2017). Giving kids an allowance: What you need to know. Retrieved April 8, 2018, from https://www.babycenter.com/0_giving-kids-an-allowance-what-you-need-to-know_10304079.bc.

George Lucas Educational Foundation (April 1, 2009). Redefining Smart: Multiple Intelligences. Retrieved January 28, 2018, from https://www.edutopia.org/multiple-intelligences-introduction.

Beekun, R. (December 01, 2011). Follow the Sunna of the Prophet (ﷺ): How Exercise Benefits the Brain and Overall Performance. Retrieved March 19, 2018, from https://theislamicworkplace.com/2011/12/01/follow-the-sunna-of-the-prophet-s-how-exercise-benefits-the-brain-and-overall-performance/.

Hoerr, T. R. (2000). Chapter 1. The Theory of Multiple Intelligences. Retrieved March 20, 2018, from http://www.ascd.org/publications/books/100006/chapters/The-Theory-of-Multiple-Intelligences.aspx

Chapter Three
Supporting Speech & Language Development
Weronika Ozpolat

Communication is one of the most important skills humans develop. It is a skill that is crucial for survival as well as being a means to interact with others and make friends. Without it you would not be able to call for help, order a coffee or tell someone you love them. The ability to communicate so sophisticatedly sets us apart from other animals. No other animal has the ability to communicate like we do. Allah made us unique.

"And of His signs is the creation of the heavens and the earth and the diversity of your languages and your colours. Indeed in that are signs for those of knowledge." (Quran 30:22)

Speech and language development is the process of acquiring our system of communication. This process starts even before birth as babies have the ability to hear at 18 weeks gestation when they are still inside the womb. Therefore, by the time they are born, they will have already listened to hundreds of sounds and now it is time for them to learn how to decipher them. Over the coming years, babies will become better and better at understanding the language spoken around them, and then they will begin to speak themselves.

It is important to understand the difference between speech and language; they are not the same thing. Speech is the sounds that are spoken and the way in which they are spoken. Language is the actual words and their meanings. It also encompasses all the different components of speech which is what we call grammar.

In this chapter, I will give you an insight into not only typical speech and language development but also what can happen when something differs from the norm. I will inform you about speech and language delay and other communication issues. I will talk about bilingualism and what kind of an impact that can have on your child's speech and language, if any. I will then give you some ideas to help with your child's speech and language development.

MILESTONES

Just as with all types of child development, there are guidelines as to the typical ages for speech and language development. When a baby is born, she is unable to produce many sounds so you will not hear much other than crying in the first few weeks. Crying is their method of communication and is their way of telling you that they need something. By eight weeks old, you can expect your baby to make some cooing sounds which are produced at the back of the throat and are often accompanied by a vowel sound. They will begin to smile at around 4-6 weeks old and, soon after, they may begin to laugh.

From 3-6 months, babies cries are differentiated. You may begin to recognise that their different cries represent different needs. For example, they may cry differently when they are hungry to when they are hurt. They start to turn their head towards voices and begin to recognise their own name. They may begin to imitate facial expressions that they see.

They start babbling which involves consonant and vowel sound combinations and they may appear to be trying to interact with adults.

At 6-9 months, they can start to use gestures and exchange gestures with adults. This is why baby signing has become popular; babies are able to produce signs using their hands before they are able to communicate via talking. They may begin to imitate repetitive sounds that they hear. Babbling becomes variegated, meaning they are starting to produce different combinations of sounds together and not just repetitive ones. They may begin to show understanding of simple commands such as "Come here," and may wave in response to a "Goodbye."

At 9-12 months, a baby may say his first word but it is also normal for them to produce their first word after 12 months. The first words produced at this stage tend to be "Mama" or "Dada" which are easy — as well as important — words for them to produce. They may say one or two words spontaneously. They start to imitate more consonant and vowel combinations and may also imitate the names of familiar objects. They begin to use jargon, speech-like utterances which sounds like speech but without any meaningful words. When producing jargon they may sound like they are trying to have a proper conversation!

Around 12 months is when we expect to see the emergence of the first word and they may be able to produce a few words by the time they get to 15 months. They may shake their head to communicate "No" and may imitate the sounds of animals as well as the sounds they hear other children make. They start to use real words within their jargon. They also begin to take turns during play or conversations.

Between 15-18 months, you will begin to notice that they are producing a few more words. Speech is used increasingly in place of gestures and they may begin to ask, "What's that?"

They also start to ask for "More."

From 18-21 months, they begin to understand more commands and action words. They may begin to identify pictures when you name them. They begin to imitate household chores and start to lead adults to an object that they desire. They may even imitate 2-3 words that they hear and engage in "adult-like" dialogue.

Around 21-24 months is when you can expect your toddler to understand a lot more and be able to follow simple 2-step commands. They begin to refer to themself by name and may begin to start putting two words together as well as regularly saying new words. By the age of 24 months, children can have a vocabulary of between 50-200 words!

As you can see, there is a huge variation there and all children are different.

From 24 months onwards is when you can really start to see a language explosion! Toddlers are regularly saying two word phrases and are beginning to produce three word phrases.

They start to use action words.

During the second year they learn to put more words together and talk to other children. They answer to yes/no questions correctly and start to use plurals and prepositions (on, in, under, etc.) By the age of three years old, you can expect your child to be talking in sentences, counting to three and following 3-step commands.

Age	Speech and Language Development
0-3 months	• Cooing, crying, smiling and laughing
3-6 months	• Differentiated crying • Turns head towards voices • Begins to recognise own name • Imitates facial expressions • Repetitive babbling – repeating vowel and consonant sound combinations
6-9 months	• Starts to use gestures • Begins to imitate repetitive sounds they hear • Variegated babbling – different combinations of sounds • Begins to show understanding of simple commands • Waves in response to "Goodbye."
9-12 months	• May say first word • Starts to imitate more consonant and vowel combinations • Imitates names of familiar objects

	- Begins to use jargon – speech-like utterances
12-15 months	- First words - Shakes head to communicate "No." - Imitates animal sounds - Uses real words within their jargon - Begins to take turns during play or conversations
15-18 months	- Starting to produce more words - Speech used increasingly instead of gesture - May begin to ask, "What's that?" or "More."
18-21 months	- Understands more commands and action words - May identify pictures when you name them - Imitates household chores - May lead an adult to an object that they desire - May imitate 2-3 words that they hear - Engages in jargon – adult-like dialogue

21-24 months	• Increased understanding • Able to follow 2-step commands • Refers to self by name • Begins to put 2 words together • Regularly says new words • At 24 months they should produce 50-200 words
24 months +	• Language explosion • Regularly produces 2 word phrases and start to produce 3 word phrases • Starts to use action words • Talks to other children • Answers yes/no questions correctly • Starts to use plurals and prepositions (on, in, under, etc.)
36 months	• Talks in sentences • Puts three words together • Counts to three.

Table 3.1 Speech and Language Milestones from 0-36 Months.

PARENT'S ROLE IN SUPPORTING SPEECH AND LANGUAGE DEVELOPMENT

The way you interact with your baby will help her develop and reach these milestones.

1. Respond to Your Baby's Vocalisations

For every coo and babble that you hear, respond with speech sounds. This will help your child to develop these sounds into speech. Your child needs to hear human speech in order to be able to copy and produce it.

2. Use Child-Directed Speech (CDS)

Modify your speech to short sentences using a high-pitched, exaggerated expression. Make sure that you clearly pronounce each word and have distinct pauses between speech segments. Repeat new words in a variety of contexts. This type of speech will aid your child's language comprehension.

3. Establish Joint Attention

Follow your baby's line of vision to establish joint attention. Once you see what baby is looking at, comment on what baby sees. This will help her to label and give names to things in her environment. This will also help your child with language comprehension and vocabulary development.

4. Engage Your Toddler in Conversations Regularly

The more you have conversations with your child, the more she will use her words to respond and this helps in the development of language and speech. This includes reading to her, joining in her activities — such as during her play — and even when you are feeding her or changing her. It is the everyday conversations that contribute to language and speech development.

SPEECH AND LANGUAGE DELAY

Sometimes a child's speech and language does not emerge in a way that we typically expect. One of the most common difficulties is speech and language delay. The cause of this is largely unknown, however, some children have a speech and language delay as part of an underlying condition such as autism or Rett Syndrome. Others simply speak later than their peers but they often catch up by the time they start school.

So why does a child have delayed speech? Well, some children just start to speak later than others, just as some children start to walk later. If you are concerned about your child's speech and language development, the first thing to check is your child's hearing.

1. Hearing Difficulties

If they have a hearing impairment, this may be the reason they are talking late. If they can't hear it, they are not going to learn to understand language or produce sounds and words. Hearing impairment is usually picked up quickly as all babies are screened for it soon after birth.

These children may go on to get hearing aids or cochlear implants.

However, there are lots of children who have normal hearing at birth but then develop glue ear at some point during the first few years of life. This can affect their hearing and, therefore, their speech and language development. Glue ear is quite common in young children. It is caused by the build up of fluid in the ear, normally after a child has had a cold. The fluid often goes away on its own, but sometimes it does not and this can cause difficulties with hearing. You may suspect your child has glue ear if you notice they do not respond when you call them or if you are repeating things to them quite often. Also, they may complain of noises being too quiet or too loud. You may not expect complaining of loud noises to be a sign of glue ear but it can be. If you suspect that your child has glue ear then you can take them for a hearing test.

2. Speech Sounds Difficulties

One of the most common difficulties I have come across in clinic, is children with speech sound difficulties. This is when children struggle to produce certain sounds. They may say "tar" instead of "car" or "dee" instead of "see."

When children are just starting to talk, their speech is not very clear. This is because it takes time for them to acquire all the different sounds they need to speak the language of their environment. There is a particular order in which speech sounds are usually acquired, starting with the consonants /p/, /b/, /m/, /n/, /t/ and /d/ between the ages of 1-2 years old and ending with /r/ and /th/ sounds between the ages of 6-8 years old. Therefore, it is not surprising that at two years old children have only 25% intelligibility.

If intelligibility does not improve over the coming years, your child may have difficulties producing some of the sounds. They may get referred to speech and language therapy and their speech sounds will be assessed.

If there are particular sounds that are causing problems, your child may be invited for a course of speech and language therapy. This will involve your child playing games and interacting with a speech and language therapist in order to practise producing the sound or sounds they are finding difficult.

3. Language Delay

Language delay is different from speech delay because it is to do with the actual words and their meanings rather than how the words are produced. A child may have a difficulty with receptive language. Receptive is another word for understanding. So a child who has receptive language delay has a difficulty understanding the language he hears.

Some children have difficulties with expressive language. This is the language they are producing themselves, in other words, talking. If a child does not produce many words, at least 50 words by 24 months, they could have a language delay. A child may not only produce a small number of words, they may also have difficulties joining the words together to make sentences. As we have seen previously, children begin to join two words together at around two years old. By the time they reach their third birthday they can put a number of words together into short, or sometimes quite long, utterances. If a child is not doing this, they may have language delay.

Another difficulty a child may have is with specific aspects of grammar. They may find verbs difficult, for example, or pronouns. All these difficulties are types of language delay.

AUTISM

Autism Spectrum Disorder, or ASD, is a term used to describe a range of behaviours. ASD is a neurological disorder that affects social communication, interaction and imagination. Children with ASD may or may not have speech and language delay. Around half of autistic people have learning difficulties and half do not. Those that do have learning difficulties are said to have low functioning autism and those that do not are said to have high functioning autism.

Among those with high functioning autism are a group of people who are said to have Asperger Syndrome. The main difference between those with high functioning autism and Asperger syndrome is that children with high functioning autism most likely had speech and language delay and those with Asperger syndrome did not. However, in some places – such as America – the Asperger's syndrome classification has now been removed and all high-functioning individuals are said to have high-functioning autism.

1. Social Communication

Children with autism have many difficulties with communication. Not only may they have difficulties with speech and language, they may not even have a desire to communicate. They also have difficulties interacting with others, starting and maintaining conversations and making friends. They also have difficulties deciphering facial expressions and understanding emotions and, because of this, they may find it difficult to work out whether someone is happy or sad, for example.

Echolalia is another sign of autism. This is when children repeat things that they have heard rather than produce unique utterances. They may repeat what you have said back to you or ask the same questions over and over again.

Children with autism often have their own special interests and they may talk about these obsessively regardless of the interests of the listener.

2. Imagination

They also have difficulties understanding the knowledge and beliefs of other people. Because of this, they may say things that you might not understand because they do not realise that you do not have the same knowledge as them. For example, if they went to the park at the weekend and had a strawberry ice cream, they may think that you know this even if you weren't there. Next time you see them at the park you may ask, "Which ice cream would you like?" They may reply, "The same one I had on Saturday," leaving you perplexed. You may notice autistic children using ambiguous utterances such as this and wonder what they mean.

Children with autism may have difficulties understanding idioms and will take things literally. I once heard of a child who, when moving house, heard his father say, "We've got everything but the kitchen sink." So what did he proceed to do? Go and get the kitchen sink!

Autistic children may have obsessive interests. I once saw a 2-year-old child who was completely obsessed with cars and knew the names for all the different makes of cars. He could immediately tell you if a car was a Vauxhall, Renault or any other make as soon as he saw it.

3. Social Interaction

Autistic children often find it difficult to understand non-verbal behaviours such as eye-contact, gestures and facial expressions. Therefore, they may not interact in usual or appropriate ways. They may stand too close or may touch you inappropriately. They may make little or no eye contact when they are talking to you. They may not understand the different ways in which you communicate with different people such as the difference between communicating with a friend and communicating with a police officer or teacher.

STUTTERING

Stuttering, or stammering as it is known in British English, is a psychogenic voice disorder which means that it has a psychological basis. It is common among young children between 2-5 years of age. One in 20 young children have a stammer, however, 75% of children grow out of it. Of those that have a stammer that persists after the age of five, treatment can be helpful. Treatment will consist of different strategies, such as breathing techniques, which will help reduce anxiety about talking.

BILINGUALISM

With two-thirds of the world's population speaking more than one language, it seems reasonable to think that bilingualism is achievable. Research has increasingly proven that there are many benefits to being bilingual. Bilingualism increases cognitive abilities such as attention and flexibility. You may also be better at learning other languages at school. Then there are the practical benefits. If you are able to understand more than one language, you are able to have access to more information, different experiences and different ways of life. It may enable you to have more work-related opportunities or perhaps it might enable you to communicate with family members in different countries.

Parents are often worried that speaking more than one language to their child could lead to them developing problems such as speech and language delay. However, they needn't worry as this is not the case.

Research shows that there is a very slight delay for bilinguals; 2-3 months. As the variation of monolingual children may be a few months either side of the typical milestones, this means that bilingual children do not have a significant chance of having delayed speech and language.

So what if a bilingual child does have delayed speech and language? Just as monolingual children may have a speech and language delay, bilingual children may also have a delay. However, if a bilingual child has speech and language delay it is not because they are bilingual. Chances are they would have had a speech and language delay if they were monolingual.

Many people will think their bilingual child has a delay if they are not saying as many words in the majority language as their monolingual peers. This may be because bilinguals will have their vocabulary split over the two languages. Therefore, while a monolingual may say 100 words in their one language at the age of 2 years old, a bilingual child may say 50 words in each language. Therefore, it can appear that they know less words while in fact, they know the same amount but they have half the words in one language and half in the other.

Another worry parents of bilinguals have, is when their children mix the two languages when they are speaking. This is a natural phenomenon called code mixing or code switching. Code switching is when you say a phrase in one language and then switch to another language for the next phrase. Code mixing is when you mix the two languages within a phrase. Bilingual children are very likely to do this and may not learn that the languages are separate until the age of 3 or 4 years old. After this age, they learn how to separate the languages and when they should speak each language and with whom.

When children get older, code mixing is actually a sign of fluency so do not worry if your child continues to do this. Code mixing is governed by rules. In order to code mix, you need to know when and where you can make a switch according to each languages grammatical elements. Therefore, it is a sign of fluency. You need to be pretty fluent in the languages in order to know when and where you can mix them.

To conclude, bilingualism does not cause a significant language delay. In fact, bilingualism has many benefits.

If you are part of a multilingual family, embrace this and bring your children up to speak more than one language. It is recommended that you speak your first language with your child. This is because if you speak a language to your child that you are not very fluent in, they could learn grammatical and lexical errors from you. Young children cope very well with acquiring two or more languages from birth. It is so much easier for them to learn languages when they are young so do not miss this opportunity!

ACTIVITIES TO HELP YOUR CHILD'S SPEECH AND LANGUAGE DEVELOPMENT

In this section I will tell you about some activities you can do with your child to help their speech and language development.

<u>Ways to Improve Listening and Attention</u>

When a speech and language therapist assesses a child for speech and language delay, one of the first things they will check is their hearing. As I said before, if they are not hearing it, we cannot expect them to understand or produce it themselves. Here are some activities you can do to practise listening skills.

1. Frog Game

The child has to listen to instructions and do certain actions for each instruction. The actions and instructions are:

In the pond – both hands on the floor

On the bank – both hands on lap

Up a tree – hands by shoulders

High up a tree – both hands in the air

The adult says, "The frog is…" followed by one of the instructions. They will then watch to see if the child does the correct action to go with the instruction.

2. Instrument Match

You will need pairs of instruments i.e. two drums, two shakers, two triangles, etc.

The adult has their instruments out of sight of the child, perhaps hidden under a sheet. The adult plays one of the instruments. The child listens and plays the same instrument. This can be increased in difficulty by the adult playing a pattern of instruments and the child having to repeat the pattern.

Ways to Improve Speech and Language

If a child has speech and language delay, there are a number of strategies you can use to help them.

1. Listen to Your Child

When babies are learning to talk, they need to know that what they are saying is meaningful. Therefore, when you hear your young child attempting to speak, it is really important that you listen to what they are saying. Listening to your child and responding in some way, either verbally or non-verbally (by touching or kissing them,) has a significant impact on their speech and language development. You can do this very early on when they are just starting to babble. Whenever you hear them say any sounds, respond with a simple word or phrase, or simply touch them. By doing this, they will begin to realise that their attempts to speak are important because speaking gets a response from you. This will encourage them to keep making noises and, eventually, start to talk.

2. Give Choices

Children love to have the opportunity to make decisions for themselves. Make sure you are giving your child lots of choices throughout the day. When you speak, hold the object near your mouth as this will direct the child's gaze to your mouth and will prompt them to look at how you are producing the words. At snack time ask, "Would you like the apple or the orange?" During play time ask, "Would you like to play with the cars or the blocks"' At bedtime ask, "Would you like the Thomas book or the Elmer book?"

You get the picture. The important thing is to get your child communicating with you. It may just be a point at first; they may just reach towards the object they desire. Do not be put off by this, this is communication after all! They may vocalise, say the first sound of the word or say something unintelligible. Do not worry, this is a good start.

3. Running Commentary

Babies and young children learn language by listening to it in their surrounding environment. Therefore, make sure you are talking as much as possible and giving them the chance to hear it! When you are getting them dressed in the morning, "Your socks go on your feet." When you are making the breakfast say, "I'm pouring the milk into the bowl."

4. Use Short, Simple Phrases

It may be useful to talk to them in shorter phrases than you are used to. This will help with their understanding and also help them to pick up and learn key words. Instead of saying, "I've told you a thousand times not to hit other children because you could hurt them and it's very naughty. You are in so much trouble now. Why don't you ever listen to me when I'm talking to you?" Try saying, "No hitting. Hitting hurts. Please listen to me."

5. Expand on What They Say

If your child is still at the one word stage and you are trying to help them move on from this, try expanding on what you hear them say. If they say "car," you say, "The big blue car" or "The car is driving." If they say "apple," you say, "Would you like an apple?" or "You are eating your apple" or "Apples are tasty."

Although you are trying to expand what they are saying, try not to use so much language that they become overwhelmed.

Whatever you do, do not force your child to repeat a word or phrase or copy what you are saying. That can be very frustrating and upsetting for a child who is trying their hardest to talk. The point is to model what the correct word or phrase is and, hopefully, by listening to you they will pick it up. Model the desired speech and language. Be a communication role model for your child.

Games for Understanding

1. Shopping

Have a selection of objects to "buy" and a shopping basket. Ask your child to go shopping and buy you a few items. See if they buy the correct ones. Start with asking for two things and gradually increase the number.

2. Actions with Teddy

Get a teddy or doll and ask your child to use it to do actions. Practise verbs by asking them to "brush teddy's hair" or "make dolly jump." It is also a useful way to practise prepositions. Ask them to place teddy on, under or behind the table or chair.

Games for Speaking

There are so many games you can play with your child to help their speech and language skills. Here are some of my favourites.

1. Treasure Hunt

Children love hide-and-seek games. Hide flashcards or objects around the room when your child is not looking. Perhaps send them out of the room while you do this. Call them back in and ask them to find the cards or objects. When they find them, ask them if they can say the letter or word shown on the card.

2. Matching Pairs

Get two sets of the same flashcards. Turn them all over so they are face down. Take turns to turn over the cards, two at a time, and see if you can find a matching pair. Each time you turn over a card, say the word or letter printed on it.

<u>Ways to Encourage Bilingualism</u>

Although learning two or more languages from birth can be easy for children, it often becomes increasingly difficult to maintain all of the languages as they get older. Here are some tips to help you.

1. Speak the Minority Language at Home

If you are able to speak the minority language to your child at home, this really is the best way to ensure they have a good knowledge of it. When children are surrounded by **the minority language in the home**, this will create an excellent environment for the acquisition of that language. Read it on my blog.

2. Speak the Minority Language at Certain Times

If you are not able to speak the minority language all the time, **another method is to use it at certain times**. This could be on certain days of the week — Turkish Tuesdays, for example — or at a certain time of day, such as mealtimes. Think about your family routine and what works best for you. Read it on my blog. Read it also on my blog.

3. Read

Reading is an excellent way to improve language skills, not only books, but also newspapers and magazines or blog articles too. If you cannot find books in the minority language, the internet is an excellent way to find reading materials in the target language. Look at online newspapers or blogs. Older children can print out articles to read or use them to practise translation. Highlight words and phrases to remember and write notes in the margins. It can be helpful to have a small notebook to write down new words or phrases you come across.

4. Use Language Learning Resources

There are many different resources you can purchase for learning a language at home. There are workbooks, flashcards and apps. You may even be able to find board games, that have a language element, in the target language. Try to find resources that are fun and hold your child's interest. This way, they are much more likely to be motivated to use them and learn.

5. Arrange Play Dates With Other Children Who Speak the Language

If you know some other families who speak the same language then make opportunities for your children to get together outside of class time to socialise. Encourage them to practise the minority language together. It's always more fun to learn with friends!

6. Watch TV in the Minority Language

I am not normally a fan of screen time but when it comes to screen time in the minority language, this can be a great way of improving language skills. If you want to use this as a method for learning the minority language, make sure your children are not too young. Children will not get much out of watching programs in the minority language until they are at least three years old. Before the age of three, it is much more important for them to acquire the language through social interaction with others.

I hope this chapter has given you an understanding of the speech and language issues that can affect children and the strategies mentioned have given you some ideas to help you to help your children in the future.

Chapter Four
Promoting Motor Skills
Nabila Ikram

Children are naturally inquisitive little beings. From grasping a caregiver's finger for the first time to learning how to swing from the monkey bars at a playground, children are constantly learning from the environment around them. As some like to say, children are tiny scientists who are constantly guessing, testing, failing or succeeding, and then repeating the process.

Physical changes in early childhood are accompanied by rapid changes in the child's cognitive and language development. Therefore, all the domains of child development are interconnected and are necessary for the proper growth of one another.[1] Children learn in many different ways and each child has his own pace of learning. To continue the scenario of the scientist, children need opportunities to hypothesize, experiment, observe, and draw conclusions. The most

---

[1] *Children's Developmental Domains.* Child Health Explanation. http://www.childhealth-explanation.com/developmental-domains.html

natural way for them to do so is by simply playing.

PLAY: AN ESSENTIAL PART OF CHILDHOOD

In modern research, the theory of play-based learning has gained great significance and more early childhood curriculums around the world are embracing it. The theory calls for allowing young children to learn through play, instead of exposing them to a structured learning environment at a young age. It is believed that play allows children to learn various socio-emotional skills needed to establish a strong foundation on which future learning can be built. 2

However, before delving deeper into some of the ideas of play-based learning, let's take a look at how parenting, education, and childhood are viewed in Islam:

Some commonly-cited *ahadith*, such as the one mentioned below, often point to how the Prophet ﷺ did not reprimand children for playing, even when they were possibly interrupting acts of worship:

It was narrated from 'Abdullah bin Shaddad, that his father said, "The Messenger of Allah ﷺ came out to us for one of the nighttime prayers, and he was carrying Hasan or Husain. The Messenger of Allah ﷺ came forward and put him down, then he said the Takbir and started to pray. He prostrated during his prayer and made the prostration lengthy. My father said, 'I raised my head and saw the child on the back of the Messenger of Allah ﷺ while he was prostrating, so I went back to my prostration.' When the Messenger of Allah ﷺ finished praying, the people said, 'O Messenger of Allah, you prostrated during the prayer for so long that we thought that something had happened or that you were receiving a revelation.' He said, 'No such thing happened. But my son was riding on my back and I did not like to disturb him until he had enough.'" (Sunan Al-Nasai, 1141)

---

[2] *Defining Play-based Learning.* Daniels, Erica & Angela Pyle. OISE University of Toronto, Canada. 2018. http://www.child-encyclopedia.com/play-based-learning/according-experts/defining-play-based-learning

The Prophet ﷺ also encouraged games and sports:

"Everything that is not from the remembrance of Allah is vain talk and play, except if it is one of four: a man playing with his wife, a man training his horse, a man going to obtain his needs, or a man's learning how to swim." (al Jami as Saghir, 4534)

Ai'sha, may Allah be pleased with her, says, "I competed with the Messenger of Allah ﷺ (in running) and overtook him. Later, when I had put on some weight, I once again competed with him, but this time he overtook me and said, 'We're even now'." (Ahmad, 11, 16(p26),17)

We also learn that Islam views child development and parenting in three phases of seven years:

Ali ibn Abi Talib ؓ is reported to have said, "Play with them for the first seven years (of their life); then teach them for the next seven years; then advise them for the next seven years (and after that)."

For the first seven years, the early childhood years, the focus is on teaching children social skills, manners and etiquette, through playing and simply letting children be children. For the next seven years, more formal education is encouraged, both academically and spiritually. The final seven years, or adolescence, parents are encouraged to involve their children in their affairs by keeping them by their side, asking for their opinions, and respecting them as autonomous individuals, while still advising them with wisdom, all of which prepares them for the real world.[3]

Regarding the early childhood years, interestingly, modern research is beginning to realise the benefits of play and delaying structured schooling, or academics. A popular case study is Finland. Finland's educational system has consistently ranked globally in the top tier of quality output for more than a decade. Countries around the world

---

[3] *The Responsibility of Children + 21 Theory*. Ilm Fruits. 2014. http://ilmfruits.com/2014/the-responsibility-of-children-21-theory/

have been studying Finland's heavily research-based system in hopes of replicating their practices. Some of the observations that have been made about the Finnish system are **4:**

They place utmost importance on the preschool, or the early childhood, years. Therefore, they invest significant funds and resources to properly research and develop the curriculum.

Students do not start academics until they are seven years old. Until the age of seven, students are engaged in creative play, a mix of free, natural play and teacher-directed play, to teach emotional well-being, cooperation, and other social and self-regulatory skills. 5

Physical play is highly emphasized with students receiving 15 minutes of recess for every 45 minutes of instruction.

From this we can see for ourselves that what Islam says and what modern research is proving is one and the same.

MOTOR DEVELOPMENT

When it comes to early childhood, you may recall some of your fondest memories from your adventures in the backyard, playing board games, recess in the playground, or playing sports. Therefore, play, in all its forms, has a significant role in early childhood. Furthermore, physical play impacts one of the most obvious domains of development in young children; motor development.

Motor development is split into two categories: gross motor skills and fine motor skills. As the name indicates, fine motor skills refers to more precise physical skills, such as a baby grabbing a rattle, a toddler

---

[4] *8 reasons Finland's education system puts the US model to shame.* Weller, Chris. 2017. http://www.businessinsider.com/finland-education-beats-us-2017-5?r=UK&IR=T#8-college-tuition-is-free-8

[5] *No grammar schools, lots of play: the secrets of Europe's top education system.* Butler, Patrick. 2016.
https://www.theguardian.com/education/2016/sep/20/grammar-schools-play-europe-top-education-system-finland-daycare

feeding himself with a spoon, or a preschooler properly holding a pencil. Gross motor skills are the larger skills required for everyday mobility and tasks and require the use of larger muscle groups, such as in rolling over, walking, jumping, and picking up larger objects.

There are two sequences that motor development follows. The first is the head to tail sequence which means that the control of the head takes place first, then the trunk and arms, and finally, the legs. The second sequence starts from the centre of the body moving outwards so the head, trunk and arms are fully controlled before the hands and fingers.

While each child is unique and develops at his or her own pace, generally, most children reach certain milestones in each stage or age group.

1. Fine Motor Skills Development

Fine motor control starts with reaching and grasping at objects. Your newborn will try to reach for things dangled in front of her but will not make contact due to a lack of control of her arms. At 3 months, her reaching will be more accurate and she will start to use the ulnar grasp which is where the fingers close against the palm. At 4 to 5 months, your baby can hold an object and transfer it from one hand to the other. Towards the end of the first year, your infant can use the pincer grasp, which is the forefinger and the thumb hold, to pick up and hold objects.

Age	Fine Motor Skill
Newborn	Prereaching
3-4 months	Ulnar grasp
4-5 months	Transfer object from one hand to the other

9 months	Pincer grasp

Table 5.1 Fine Motor Development

2. Gross Motor Skills Development

At 6 weeks, your baby can hold her head up when she is held upright. She will start to roll from her side to her back at 2 months and from 4 months, she will be able to roll from her back to her side. At 7 months, your baby will start to sit by herself and to crawl. One month later, she will be able to pull herself up to stand. From 11 months, your toddler will begin to stand by herself and then will start to walk. Around 16 months, she will be able to walk upstairs with your help and will start to jump in place at 23 months.

As your baby grows, her head becomes gradually smaller and her legs longer. The centre of gravity moves from the head to the torso, making balancing much easier for your toddler. Your 2 year old can now walk smoothly and steadily. They can even jump, hop, throw and catch, but not yet flexibly.

From 3 to 4 years of age, your child can jump and hop much more flexibly but throwing and catching is still constrained. Pedalling and steering the tricycle is much easier as compared to the previous year of just pushing it with the feet and limited steering. Walking up the stairs with alternating feet is an achievement, while going downstairs is still with one foot leading.

Between 4 years of age and 5, running, riding a tricycle and walking downstairs are mastered. Throwing and catching are almost perfected. Galloping and skipping, which are usually done with one foot, are developing.

From 5 to 6 years of age, throwing, catching, galloping and skipping have matured. Your child can now trade the tricyle for a bicycle with training wheels.

Between 7 and 12 years of age, your child will increase speed and distance in running, jumping, throwing and batting. Dribbling a ball will develop and change from a slapping to a continuous, even stroke.

Age	Gross Motor Skill
6 weeks	• Hold head up when held
2 months	• Roll from side to back
4 months	• Roll from back to side
7 months	• Sit alone • Crawl
8 months	• Pull to stand
11 months	• Stand alone • Walk
16 months	• Walk upstairs with help
23 months	• Jump in place
2 years	• Walk smoothly and steadily • Jump, hop, throw • and catch but not yet flexibly • Push tricycle with feet

3-4 years	• Jump and hop flexibly • Throw and catch constrained • Pedal and steer tricycle easily • Walk upstairs with alternating feet but going downstairs with one foot leading
4-5 years	• Run, ride tricycle • and walk downstairs mastery • Throw and catch almost prefect • Gallop and skip with one foot
5-6 years	• Throw, catch, gallop • and skip matured • Ride bicycle with training wheels
7-12 years	• Run, jump, throw • and bat with increasing speed, distance and accuracy • Dribble a ball from slapping to a continuous, even stroke.

Table 5.2 Gross Motor Development

ACTIVITIES TO PROMOTE MOTOR DEVELOPMENT

Early childhood can be split into the following stages: Newborn to 1 year, 1 year to 3 years, 3 years to 5 years, and 5 years to 8 years. Below are some family-budget-friendly activities that are beneficial for your child's motor development at each of these stages.

Newborn – 1 year:

Tummy Time

Tummy time is an essential part of an infant's motor development.6 It takes effort and whole muscle groups for your baby to lie on the tummy and then lift his or her head in an attempt to see the surrounding world. Tummy time not only helps with head control and strengthening the back, it also encourages your baby to learn how to roll over; the first step to becoming mobile and independent.

Tummy time can also be used to develop fine motor skills, such as by placing rattles and other toys in front of your baby. As they get older they will be tempted to pick the toys up to play, improving their grasps. Play mats are great to use for tummy time as they can encourage fine motor skill development.

1 year – 3 years:

The wonderful thing about early childhood is that anything becomes a toy and anywhere becomes a play area. At this age, your child is in full exploration mode and, therefore, no fancy toys or gadgets are necessary. Rather, everyday household items can become opportunities for incredible learning and development.

Loose Parts

Activities consisting of exploring, playing, or sorting loose parts are an excellent way of developing fine motor skills and other concepts, such as numeracy and color recognition. In addition, they are incredibly easy to prepare with materials that may be lying around at home, such as dry beans or pasta, pom poms, and pebbles.

In such activities, your child will be able to practice their fine motor skills by grasping and picking up the objects with their fingers at

---

[6] *Your Guide to Tummy Time.* Berk, Sheryl & Erin Smith. Parents.com. https://www.parents.com/baby/development/physical/tummy-time-guide/

times, and at other times, with spoons and scoops.

Such skills are also developed when teaching your child how to eat by themselves by giving them items such as dry cereal, cut up fruits, and cheese.

Stumbling/Toddling

This age group is also when children are learning to walk, and later, to run and jump. Encourage the development of their stability and coordination by allowing varying degrees of physical activity. An example is building an obstacle course in the living room, such as with blankets and a small pile of pillows, and a table to crawl under.

For the younger ones who may still be crawling, or have not completely independently started walking yet, create a path of different textured tiles (such as different carpet samples), or materials. Your child would practice their coordination, while also having a sensory experience as they walk across the different materials.

Remember to create a safe, child-friendly environment (i.e. no sharp edges or hard surfaces) before doing any such activities.

3 years – 5 years:

Children in this age group are perhaps the most active and daring. Harness this energy by continuing to encourage safe physical activity, while also teaching rules and boundaries. The obstacle course idea mentioned in the last age group applies here too. At this age, your child can also start playing games that consist of following directions.

Traditional Games

Games such as Simon Says; Red Light, Green Light; and a basic form of Hopscotch can all be great to introduce at this age. Not only do these games allow your child to indulge in physical play, they also teach other concepts such as a sense of self, self-regulation, and social skills.

At this age, your child will also become more experienced in skills such as holding a pencil, zipping a bag, and opening a juice box. Therefore, these are also learning opportunities that could be incorporated throughout the day.

<u>5 years – 8 years:</u>

In the pre-K+ years, children are becoming mentally, emotionally, and physically ready for school. Even if a family chooses to homeschool, a child around this age is becoming ready for more structure in a daily routine and to start engaging with academics. Play and motor development are still essential at this age and opportunities to play freely and naturally should be plenty.

Writing & Art

Colouring and painting are essential activities even for the younger groups, as is discussed further below, but at this age your child can become more interested and inclined towards activities such as writing their names, drawing different scenes or even their own stories, and various other crafts. Such activities continue to help develop fine motor skills, while also developing other areas, such as literacy.

At this age, it is also a good time to introduce your child to structured games and sports, such as soccer, basketball, gymnastics, and swimming.

<u>Ageless Activities:</u>

While the above activities are broken down by age groups, the fact of the matter is that any activity can be modified to meet the developmental level for each child. One thing to remember is that every child is different. Especially in the early childhood years, the range and pace of development and ability is vast. As each child is moving towards the expected milestones, it can be common to see one child be highly advanced in one skill and very well "behind" in another. Therefore, your child should not be compared and, instead, each child should be encouraged to develop at his or her natural pace.

With that in mind, there are a few activities (or materials) that are simply ageless. These materials are incredibly versatile and can be used to create a wide range of activities for any age group. They provide excellent sensory and problem-solving opportunities that satisfy the inner scientist (or Olympian) in every child.

Some of These Activities Are:

Water/Sensory Play

Materials such as water and sand, along with a couple of cups and scoops, can provide some of the most satisfying sensory experiences for your child. Paint is also an excellent art material to include in many different types of sensory activities.

Nature Play

Let your child play outdoors with minimal adult involvement. By allowing them to play in the dirt, in the grass, observe bugs and insects, dissect flowers, throw sticks and stones, watch birds etc. The list of science and math lessons your child can receive by simply playing in the backyard is endless.

Parks & Playgrounds

The biggest obstacle course is the one at the local park. Take your child out to playgrounds regularly so they can release their energy in highly stimulating ways, whether it is swinging, sliding, climbing, running, jumping, or more.

Conclusion

Early childhood is a time of wide-eyed wonder, natural curiosity, and intense energy. As your child passes through each stage of development with expected milestones at each stage, you have plenty of opportunities to provide him or her with enriching learning opportunities. It is highly beneficial for you to keep in mind that play has been encouraged in the Islamic tradition, as well as in modern research. By allowing your child to engage in various forms of play, he or she can develop a strong foundation for future learning and growth as a whole individual who is competent and confident physically, emotionally, and spiritually.

Chapter Five
Nurturing Healthy Physical Growth
Afshan Mohammed

There are two growth spurts. One occurs in the very first year of life where height and weight gain increases rapidly. After which they slow down until the onset of puberty. Growth in height and weight increases rapidly once again during this adolescent growth spurt. Girls generally go through the adolescent growth spurt earlier than boys.

With these growth spurts, children need the right nutrition to nurture a healthy body. If children don't get the right nutrition, it could lead to malnutrition or obesity and other health issues.

INFLUENCS ON PHYSICAL GROWTH

1. Nutrition

Allah ﷻ mentions in his holy Book:

"O you who have believed, eat from the good things which We have provided for you and be grateful to Allah if it is Him that you worship." (Quran 2:172)

Allah ﷻ adds :

"This day, good things have been made lawful for you." (Quran 5:5)

Allah ﷻ uses the word "tayyib," defined as "good" in English. This shows that not only should we aim to eat and feed our kids halal foods but also pure and *tayyib* foods.

Some good foods are mentioned by Allah ﷻ. He ﷻ states:

"He is the One who made the earth a bed for you, and the sky a roof, and sent down water from the sky, then brought forth with it fruits, as a provision for you. So, do not set up parallels to Allah when you know." (Quran 2:22)

Specifically, He ﷻ mentions, "He is the One who sent down water from the heavens. Then We brought forth with it vegetation of all kinds. Then from it We brought grains set upon one another. From the palm-trees, from their spathes, come forth the low hanging bunches. (We produce) vineyards and the olive and the pomegranate, either similar or not similar to each other. Look at its fruit when it bears fruit, and at its ripening. Surely, in all this there are signs for the people who believe." (Quran 6:99)

Fruits and Vegetables

Allah ﷻ mentions fruits in many *ayats* of the Quran showing the importance of fruit as a form of food for us today. In the above *ayat*, he also mentions greens and grains.

Most fruits are low in fat, calories, and sodium. And no fruits have cholesterol. Eating fruits and vegetables as children helps reduce the risk of a heart attack and stroke later in life. When choosing fruits and vegetables, choose the colours of the rainbow. Choosing a variety of fruits and vegetables ensures that your child gets the nutrients they need. Fruits are high in dietary fiber, which helps us stay full. Fiber also helps prevent constipation.

Dates are *sunnah* fruit, which contain a lot of fibre as well. When your baby is first born, you can do a process called *tahneek* where you take a date and chew it to make it soft and then wipe it on the roof of your baby's mouth. Be sure that the date does not go inside the baby's mouth as it's a choking hazard. Prophet Muhammad ﷺ would take a date and chew it and wipe it in many of the Sahaba's babies' mouths.

Before your baby is even born during pregnancy, you can eat dates to help with labour pain. In the Quran, when Maryam was in pain, Jibrael said to her, "...Do not grieve; your Lord has placed a stream beneath you. Shake the trunk of the palm-tree towards yourself and, it will drop upon you ripe fresh dates. So eat, drink and cool your eyes..." (Quran 19: 24-26)

Allah ﷻ has entrusted us with our bodies and our children's. It is our responsibility to take care of our bodies and our children's bodies by choosing the right food for them.

Other than fruits and vegetables, whole grains, lean meats, nuts, beans, and low-fat dairy are also healthy choices for your child.

2. Malnutrition

Malnutrition is when the body does not get enough nutrients. When we think of malnutrition, we may imagine a thin person. However, malnutrition can be in overweight or obese people too. This is why it is very important to keep your child nourished with plenty of healthy food items.

At the other extreme, over nutrition is a form of malnutrition in which a person consumes too many calories but does not eat enough nutritious foods. Mineral, vitamin, and protein deficiencies can be a result of this.

3. Overweight and Obesity

Overweight and obesity are defined as abnormal or excessive fat accumulation that presents a risk to health (World Health Organization, WHO). According to the Centre of Disease Control and Prevention (CDC), 1 in 6 children and adolescents are affected by obesity in the United States. This number is reflected in many western societies.

The prevention of obesity actually starts when you are pregnant. Eating a variety of healthy food, as mentioned above, helps prevent childhood obesity. Breastfeeding also helps prevent obesity. Encouraging physical activity and portion control also helps with preventing obesity.

Instead of trying to make your child finish all of his or her food, watch for hunger cues and fullness cues. This does not mean to waste food, but to start off by putting small amounts of food on your child's plate at a time and letting them eat until they are satisfied and not over full. If going for seconds and thirds, give them vegetables since they have lower calories and will keep them full longer. Opt for water instead of soda or juice.

The *sunnah* way of eating will also help prevent obesity. We must remember that Allah says "...eat and drink, but be not excessive. Indeed, He likes not those who commit excess." (Quran 7:31) The first thing is to eat less. How do we do this? The Prophet ﷺ said, "No man fills a container worse than his stomach. A few morsels that keep his back upright are sufficient for him. If he has to, then he should keep one-third for food, one-third for drink and one-third for his breathing." (At-Tirmidhi, 516) This is portion control the sunnah way.

YOUR BABY

1. Benefits of Breastfeeding

The first source of nutrition for a baby is breast milk. Allah ﷻ says about breastfeeding:

"Mothers (should) suckle their children for two full years, for one who wants to complete the (period of) suckling.... Now, if they want to wean, with mutual consent and consultation, there is no sin on them. And if you want to get your children suckled (by a wet-nurse), there is no sin on you when you pay off what you are to give with fairness, and fear Allah, and be assured that Allah is watchful of what you do." (Quran 2:233)

He ﷻ adds:

"We commanded man (to be good) in respect of his parents. His mother carried him (in her womb) despite weakness upon weakness, and his weaning is in two years." (Quran 31:14)

In another verse He ﷻ stated:

"...and his carrying and his weaning is (in) thirty months." (Quran 46:15)

These *ayats* put an importance on breastfeeding and mention how it is recommended for mothers to breastfeed their babies until 2 or 2 ½ years but it is not mandatory to do so if the mother is not able to.

There is a lot of benefits for both the baby and you as a mother if you breastfeed your baby. **The American Academy of Pediatrics** (AAP) currently recommends that infants should be fed breast milk exclusively for the first 6 months after birth. In addition, the **Academy of Nutrition and Dietetics** recommends exclusive breastfeeding for the first six months, and breastfeeding with nutritious foods from 6 months until at least 12 months of age.

Breastfeeding provides the best nutrition for a baby and it provides an emotional connection between you as a mother and your baby. Your baby is at a decreased risk of obesity, hypertension, ear infections, respiratory illnesses, and Sudden Infant Death Syndrome (SIDS). Breastfeeding also provides you with benefits, such as helping you to lose weight after delivery and reducing your risk of ovarian and breast cancers.

If you do not have enough breast milk to feed your baby, or if the baby is not latching properly and it is getting difficult for you to feed, then there are alternative options for you. Now there are options for you to pump milk and bottle feed your baby or you can also give your baby formula exclusively for 6 months. A dietitian, or your doctor, will be able to recommend the best formula for your baby.

2. Introducing Solids to Your Baby

As mentioned above, it is recommended to exclusively breastfeed or formula feed for the first 6 months and after the 6 months is up, then you can introduce solids. Even once solids are started, breastfeeding or formula should continue until at least one year of age.

When starting solids, introduce one new food at a time and look out for allergic reactions such as rash, vomiting or diarrhea. Start with a few spoons of food per day and let a few days pass before introducing a new food. Continue to introduce your baby to a variety of food as it is tolerated. Sometimes, multiple exposures to the same food is necessary before your baby will like a certain food. An example of some foods for a baby include: infant cereal with breast milk or formula, mashed banana, cooked and pureed squash, cooked and pureed poultry or meat.

When your baby is one year old, you can start introducing cow's milk. Continue to give your toddler a variety of fruits, vegetables, and whole grains at this time.

Once your child is one year old, he or she can eat small pieces of fruit, cooked vegetables, and soft, shredded meat, poultry or fish. Your toddler can also eat a smaller portion of the family meal.

YOUR SCHOOL-AGE CHILD

1. Dealing with Picky Eaters

To get your child involved and excited about eating certain foods, you can ask them to help you in the kitchen. For example, you can ask them to help you with cracking eggs at breakfast time or washing fruits for you at snack time.

2. School Lunches and Snacks

Luckily, school lunch has improved since the U.S. Department of Agriculture (USDA)'s Hunger-Free Kids Act of 2010. The school lunches are similar to MyPlate now. MyPlate focuses on balanced plates with fruits, vegetables, whole grains, meat and low-fat dairy. Here is a link to MyPlate:

https://www.choosemyplate.gov/MyPlate

If sending your child with a packed lunch, or if you're home schooling, try to follow the MyPlate method of giving your child food with a variety of vegetables, some whole grains, fruit, some low-fat dairy, and some meat.

When your child gets home from school, you can have healthy snacks out, such as carrots or celery sticks with low-fat ranch, peanut butter and crackers, and a variety of fruits out. A friend stated that her paediatrician suggested naming foods after unhealthy foods such as calling cucumbers "cookies" so that way your child will enjoy their snacks more. Therfore, while other kids may be eating actual cookies and your child hears about these foods often, they will have fun eating the healthy alternatives.

YOUR ADOLESCENT

It is really important to continue to encourage your adolescent or teenager to eat healthy, *zabiha halal*, and *tayyib* foods. As your child grows up, they will be going out to eat, making different friends, and they will no longer be under your influence as much as they were before. However, you can still cook healthy food for your child so they can eat a variety of food at home.

When dining out, try to choose healthy options or a healthy side option. For example, if going out for pizza, get a veggie thin crust pizza and a side salad to go with it. Make a habit of getting water instead of soda.

Body Image

In order to help your child feel comfortable in their bodies, first start off with noticing how you talk about your own body in front of them. Help your child stay healthy by encouraging healthy eating and exercise but do not focus on weight. Help them choose physical activities that they enjoy such as a sport, skating, or riding their bike, etc.

Explain to your child that Allah ﷻ has made all of us beautiful and we are beautiful in His eyes. Explain that the way the media portrays celebrities is not the right view and, from childhood, tell them the stories of the prophets, pious men and women, *sahabas*, and *sahabiat* and their strengths.

This will help show them that looks are not everything. It will also help them to see how they can use their own individual strengths, especially in Allah ﷻ 's path.

Below are a few eating disorders to look out for during the teenage years.

Anorexia Nervosa is when a person restricts their calories severely. The person may have a fear of weight gain and follow certain rules about eating. Purging after binge eating may also be present.

Bulimia Nervosa is when a person binges on food and then purges by either vomiting, using laxatives, or excessively exercising.

Binge Eating Disorder is when a person eats excessively in a short period of time.

SUNNAH ETIQUETTES OF EATING

Teach your child to eat following the *sunnah* way of eating. Start when your child is young so that it becomes a lifelong habit. Remember to model it too.

1. Begin with Bismillah

'Umar bin Abu Salamah (May Allah be pleased with him) reported: Messenger of Allah ﷺ, said to me, "Mention Allah's Name (i.e., say *Bismillah* before starting eating), eat with your right hand, and eat from what is near you." (Al-Bukhari and Muslim, 728)

2. Use the Right Hand

It was narrated from Abu Hurairah that the Prophet ﷺ said, "Let one of you eat with his right hand and drink with his right hand, and take with his right hand and give with his right hand, for Satan eats with his left hand, drinks with his left hand, gives with his left hand and takes with his left hand." (Ibn Majah, 3266 & 3390)

3. Eat or Drink Sitting Down

Qatadah Narrated From Anas, "The Prophet ﷺ prohibited that a man should drink while standing." Qatadah said, "So it was said, 'And eating?' He (Anas) said, 'That is worse.'" (At-Tirmidhi, 1879)

4. Sit Up

Abu Juhaifa Narrated, "Allah's Messenger ﷺ said, 'I do not take my meals while leaning (against something).'" (Al Bukhari, 5398)

5. Use Three Fingers

Ka'b bin Malik ؓ reported, "I saw the Messenger of Allah ﷺ eating with three fingers (i.e., the thumb, the index finger and the middle finger) and licking them after having finished the food." (Muslim, 749)

6. Eat Together

Salim bin 'Abdullah bin 'Umar said, "I heard my father say, 'I heard 'Umar bin Khattab say, 'The Messenger of Allah ﷺ said, 'Eat together and do not eat separately, for the blessing is in being together.'" (Ibn

Majah, 3287 & 3412)

7. Lick Your Fingers

Jabir ﷺ reported, "The Messenger of Allah ﷺ commanded the licking of fingers and the gleaning of the dish, saying, 'You do not know in which portion the blessing lies.'" (Muslim, 750)

PHYSICAL ACTIVITY

As mentioned above, to prevent obesity and to stay healthy, encourage your child to go out and play from the very beginning. Physical health leads to many physical, psychological and emotional benefits. It also leads to better sleep.

Enrol your child in local sports such as kindergym, soccer and basketball. When your child is young let them try out a few sessions to see if they like it. Offer a variety so your child can have choices and decide which ones they like.

As your child gets older you can encourage your child to do horse riding and archery as the Prophet ﷺ said, "...Practice archery and practice riding..." (At-Tirmidhi, 1637)

Choose activities as a family that will keep the whole family active. Have a weekend activity every week where the whole family goes cycling, walking, hiking, canoeing and so on. Not only does it keep the family active, it is also great for bonding and building relationships.

ACTIVITIES TO NURTURE A HEALTHY BODY

Below are some ideas to get your child involved in eating healthily and being active.

1. Once your baby can eat solids, try boiling fruits such as apples and pears and puree them or mash them with a spoon for a soft consistency. You can boil vegetables such as potatoes, pumpkins, sweet potatoes, spinach, carrots and peas and puree them. At first you can boil and puree them separately and feed it to your baby. Then you can experiment with different combinations to make sure that your baby has a variety of vegetables.

2. For your toddler or preschool child, since they enjoy colouring, you can give them sheets of paper with different fruits and vegetables on it and ask them to name and colour that fruit or vegetable.

3. Take your toddler or preschooler outside, blow some bubbles and let them chase and catch the bubbles. Do this several times until your child has had enough. You can then let your child blow the bubbles.

4. Lie your child on sheets of cardboard joined together to fit their length. Trace an outline of your child. Look through shopping catalogues and magazines and cut out all the fruits and vegetables. Glue them inside the body outline to make a fruit and vegetable collage. Discuss how eating lots of fruits and vegetables will help your child to grow up healthy.

5. Teach your preschooler how to handle a plastic knife to cut some soft fruits such as bananas. This way your child can help you prepare fruit salad for the family to eat. As your child gets older give them more fruits to cut and then, before you know it, your teenager can prepare fruit salad all by themselves for the whole family.

6. Your child can help you cut up fruits to put in a blender to make smoothies. Try blending frozen bananas with avocados, baby spinach leaves and coconut juice, organic milk, soy milk or almond milk. Sweeten with honey if you like. It makes a refreshing drink that your child will love. Let your child experiment with fruit combinations to find the perfect combination for them.

7. Have your adolescent or teen make a healthy meal with you such as a pizza with whole wheat pita, fresh vegetables as toppings, mozzarella cheese, and salt free tomato sauce. Let your child choose a healthy recipe each week and you can make it together.

8. Lastly as mentioned before, make sure to go out as a family to stay physically active together. Play your favourite sport together or just take a walk or jog around the neighbourhood. Kick a ball in a park or go hiking. Whatever it is, make it an outing that happens every Saturday or Sunday so it becomes a habit and everyone will look forward to it.

Chapter Six
Fostering Emotional Development
Jameela Ho

In this chapter, I will be talking about how children form attachments to their parents, how empathy develops in children and how you can help regulate your child's emotions through emotion coaching. There will be activities to help your child form a healthy attachment to you, to help your child develop empathy and for emotion coaching.

ATTACHMENT

Attachment is the strong tie that a child has with her parent. When your baby is born, if you have a responsive and nurturing relationship with her, then she will form a strong, secure attachment to you. This includes responding promptly, consistently and appropriately and holding her gently and tenderly.

If you do the opposite and engage in less physical contact, handle her awkwardly, behave in a routine manner and even resent, reject and be negative towards your child, then she will form an insecure attachment to you.

1. There are Four Phases of Attachment in Infancy

<u>From Birth to 6 Weeks</u>

This is the pre-attachment phase where your baby will recognise your smell and voice but is not yet attached to you. At this stage, you can leave your baby with anyone.

<u>At 6 Weeks to About 6 to 8 Months</u>

This is the attachment-in-the-making phase. This is when your baby will fully recognise you and will play, smile, laugh and babble with you but not others. When you respond to your baby's needs, she will start to develop a sense of trust that you will come when she needs you. Your baby will still not mind when you leave her.

During the attachment phase of about 6 to 8 months to about 18 months and two years, your child will have formed a strong attachment to you. She will start to protest when you leave her. This is called separation anxiety. At the later stage of this phase, your child will try to keep you close to her by clinging to you and sitting on you.

<u>From 18 Months to 2 Years and Above</u>

Your child will form a reciprocal relationship with you. She will protest and cling less when you leave but will instead try to persuade you to stay longer. She will request one more story or one more kiss and hug.

Age	Phase	Type of Attachment
0-6 weeks	Pre-attachment	• Not yet attached but can recognise your smell and voice.

6 weeks – 8 months	Making attachment	• Baby recognises you. • Trust is built when you respond to baby's needs
8-18 months	Attachment	• Strongly attached to you • Separation anxiety develops
18 + months	Reciprocal	• Less clingy but wants to be with you.

Table 7.1 Phases of Attachment in Infancy

The way you respond to your baby is so important and determines how your baby will respond to you, as the following section shows. These are the four ways your child can attach to you, not all of them form a healthy relationship.

1. Secure Attachment Is the Healthiest

Your baby is happy to see you and is comforted by your presence. This is formed when you are highly responsive to your child. You are affectionate when you hold your baby.

2. Avoidance Attachment

This happens if your baby is unresponsive to your presence. She treats you as she would a stranger. She will also try to get away from you. This is a result of you rejecting your baby and avoiding physical contact with her. When you have to contact her you do so with anger and intrusively such as during feeding times.

3. Resistant Attachment

Here your baby is clinging to you when you're present but when you leave and come back, she will be aggressive and angry. This is a result of you neglecting your baby. Sometimes you respond to her but most times you do not.

4. Disorganised Attachment

Your child is confused and displays contradictory behaviours in your presence. This is a result of an abusive relationship.

See the table on the next page for a summary of these attachements.

Type of Attachment	Parent Behaviour	Baby's Reaction
Secure	- Parent is highly responsive to baby's needs - Parent is affectionate when holding baby.	- Baby is happy to see parent.
Avoidance	- Parent is rejecting of baby - Avoids physical contact - Angry and intrusive.	- Baby is unresponsive to parent and tries to get away - Treats parent like a stranger.
Resistant	- Parent neglects baby - Sometimes responsive but mostly not.	- Baby is clingy to parent - Becomes aggressive and angry if parent leaves and comes back.

| Disorganised | • Parent is abusive. | • Baby is confused and displays contradictory behaviours towards parent. |

Table 7.2 Types of Attachment

2. Why Attachment Is Important For Your Child

Prophet Muhammad ﷺ understood the importance of a parent and child relationship, that it should be with kindness and physical contact. This is highlighted in the *hadith* that we should kiss our children.

Abu Hurairah ؓ narrated, "Allah's Messenger ﷺ kissed Al-Hasan ibn `Ali while Al-Aqra` ibn Habis At-Tamimi was sitting with him. Al-Aqra` said, 'I have ten children and have never kissed one of them.' The Prophet ﷺ cast a look at him and said, 'Whoever is not merciful to others will not be treated mercifully.' " (Al-Bukhari, p.34)

He ﷺ also understood the anxiety a mother should feel for her crying child. This is why he didn't prolong the prayer so the mother can concentrate on praying and then respond to her child.

Anas ibn Malik ؓ narrated, "The Prophet ﷺ said, '(It happens that) I start the prayer intending to prolong it, but on hearing the cries of a child, I shorten the prayer because I know that the cries of the child will incite its mother's passions.' " (At-Tirmidhi, 376)

Parenting is about responding to your child with love and kindness and providing physical contact. When this happens your child will have a secure attachment to you. A secure attachment leads to a healthy development for your child.

It has been found that infants who were securely attached were more effective in being independent in exploring their world by the time they're toddlers and preschoolers. By 2 years of age, these toddlers are more likely to listen and follow their mother's instructions. They also have better peer relationships and are more liked by their peers. Furthermore, they are more competent and less dependent on teachers. In contrast, insecurely attached children are likely to be more hostile with peers and are hesitant and withdrawn. At 5 to 7 years of age, they are more lonely than securely attached children.

What You Can Do

1. Spend time with your baby. Play with her. Talk to her.

2. Respond to your baby's needs immediately. When she cries, feed her, change her or pick her up. No, you are not spoiling her.

3. Provide physical contact. Kiss her, hug her and snuggle up.

EMPATHY

Empathy is the ability to place oneself in another's situation and feel what the other person is feeling. It is linked to children's emotional awareness and development.

1. Empathic Development in Children

It is believed that empathy appears at around 2 years of age, when children become self-conscious, and is when they are aware that they have a separate identity from others. They start to sense that what they feel is different to how others feel.

From 3 to 6 years of age, when children's language develops, they tend to think, reflect and use their words to respond to how others feel and console them. They become better at understanding what can cause someone to feel something and the effect of that emotion. Take this example when prekindergarten children start classes at the beginning of the school year. Adam's mother has just left him at my education centre.

"I want mummy," Adam, a 4-year-old, sits on a chair and cries.

Bilal, another 4-year-old, is sitting next to him and is playing with puzzles. Bilal turns to Adam and says, "Don't cry. Mummy is coming back."

Adam continues to cry. Bilal looks at Adam crying for a long time then tears start to fall from his eyes. He turns to me and asks, "Where's my mummy?"

In this situation, Bilal knew the cause of Adam's sadness was due to his mother not being there so he used his words to try to comfort Adam by reassuring him that Adam's mother will come back for him. However, with Adam's continued crying, Bilal began to miss his mother too.

As children's understanding of emotions grows, between 7 to 11 years of age, their empathy increases, as well as how they respond to others. Children are more aware that others can have mixed feelings and what they express may be different to what they feel.

Ten year old Amira smiles and nods her head as she listens to the teacher's explanations. "Oh I see," she says now and then. When the teacher walks away, her friend Aysha nudges her and whispers, "You didn't understand a word of that, did you?"

Aysha could read and understand Amira's confusion at what their teacher was saying and her reluctance to question the teacher further. This shows a mature understanding of the emotions of others.

From 12 years of age and onwards, they can increasingly take on the perspective of others and understand that people's emotions are continuous and they can have struggles within their everyday life. Adolescents have the ability to empathise with the poor, oppressed and sick.

Age	What your child can do
2 years	• Become self conscious
3-6 years	• Think, reflect and use words to respond to how others feel to console them
7-11 years	• Aware that others can have mixed feelings and what they express may be different to what they feel
12+ years	• Increasingly take on the perspective of others
12+ years	• Ability to empathise with the poor, oppressed and sick

Table 7.3 Empathic Development

2. Why Empathy Is Important For Your Child

Kindness is a highly valued characteristic to have in Islam. There are numerous *ahadith* on it, in which the following is one: Aisha ﷺ reported that the Messenger of Allah ﷺ said, "O Aisha, Allah is kind and He loves kindness in all matters." (Al Bukhari, 6927)

It is very difficult to be kind, though, without empathy. If your child doesn't have empathy then it will be hard for him to help, share or comfort others when they are in distress. Being Muslim means that we are helpful to everyone and everything, but especially other Muslims.

Abu Huraira ﷺ reported that the Messenger of Allah ﷺ said, "Whoever relieves the hardship of a believer in this world, Allah will relieve his hardship on the Day of Resurrection. Whoever helps ease someone in difficulty, Allah will make it easy for him in this world and in the Hereafter. Whoever covers the faults of a Muslim, Allah will cover his faults in this world and in the Hereafter. Allah helps the servant as long as he helps his brother. Whoever travels a path in search of knowledge, Allah will make easy for him a path to Paradise, for a people do not gather together in the houses of Allah, reciting the Book of Allah and studying together, except that tranquility will descend upon them, mercy will cover them, angels will surround them, and Allah will mention them to those with Him. Whoever is slow to good deeds will not be hastened by his lineage." (Muslim, 2699)

What You Can Do

1. Model Empathy

This is obvious as your child will do what you do and not what you say. To back this up, studies show that parents who are warm and have empathic concern for their children, have children who react in a concerned way to others' distress. In contrast, parents who were angry and abusive have children with similar behaviour to the distress of others.

You can use both non-verbal and verbal communications to convey empathy. A touch on the hand, a pat on the shoulder, a hug and verbal support all offer actions that your child can copy and use when he needs to comfort others. If you only offer one type of action then your child will have a limited choice to comfort others.

2. Talk about Feelings

When your child feels a big emotion do not discount it by saying, "It'll be alright" or "Don't worry about it." Validate your child's emotions and let him feel it by describing how he feels. "I can see by your red face that you're pretty mad about something." By talking about it, you are making the space for him to start talking about it and making sense of it instead of just reacting or burying it.

Even when your child is not feeling big emotions, you can help your child to talk about emotions by labelling them. "You're looking sad," "You're happy today," or "Do you feel disappointed?" or "You're feeling angry right now," will help your child to describe and say how they feel.

Take every opportunity to talk about feelings by describing how others feel as well. "She's so lonely," or "He's feeling very scared," or "Look at that disgusted look on her face," will help your child read and understand how others feel.

Another place where you can talk about feelings is when you use "I messages." "I felt very surprised when you said you wouldn't do it," and "I feel so sad when you say that to me," will help your child understand how you feel.

3. Problem Solve

When you and your child witness someone's upset or hurt don't try to fix it yourself, give your child a chance to do it. Help your child to find solutions by asking what would make the other person feel better. When your child has come up with a few alternatives then encourage him to carry out one of them. You could say, "You like to help others. Let's do it."

You are at playgroup and a child snatches a toy from another child sitting next to you. She starts to cry. Instead of ignoring it or jumping in to offer the child another toy, you say to your child, who is watching, "It's so upsetting when someone takes something away from you. What can we do to help her?" Your child might suggest to take the toy back or offer a new toy. Guide him to one solution by saying, "Let's find a really good toy to give her," and encourage your child to do it and say, "You're such a great helper!"

EMOTION COACHING

Emotion coaching is a parenting tool that teaches your child to recognise, understand and handle his feelings. I've included it here because a lot of the times, parents don't know how to handle their children's strong emotions, while their children don't know how to handle and express themselves. You can help your child regulate his emotions with this technique.

There are five steps in emotion coaching:

1. Be aware of emotions.
2. Connect with your child.
3. Listen to your child.
4. Name the emotions.
5. Find good solutions.

The first step is to be aware of your child's emotions, as well as your own. Next, encourage your child to talk about what he is feeling. Then, listen intently as he tells you how he is feeling, without judgement, so that you can understand the emotion. Next, identify and label the emotion and, finally, help your child find positive ways to handle this emotion. If his previous behavior was inappropriate, explain why.

Let me demonstrate how emotion coaching works with an example. Your child comes home and starts slamming things. This is a sign that some emotion is festering underneath. This is step one: you try to connect with your child so he can start talking to you. You come up to your child and sit near him and try to get eye contact. Once you have it, you say, "It looks like you're feeling pretty upset about something." He stares at you silently. You do not rush him. You wait until he is ready. You might say, "You must have had a tough day."

All of a sudden, he cries tears of anguish. Now is the time to listen actively, which is the third step. You listen without questioning, advising, judging, interpreting or reassuring him. You listen with understanding. You pay attention to understand what he is feeling. He tells you how the other kids in school did not pick him to be in their team for soccer, even his friends told the captain to pick the other kids first. So, he was the last one chosen.

When he stops talking, you say, "You're feeling hurt that you were the last one chosen and a bit betrayed by your friends." This is step four, no advice on what to do so he can be chosen the next time, or any reassurance that he is still the best player or even outrage on his behalf is needed. You name the emotion so he can have the language to talk about it.

In the last step, you ask your child what he can do now to ease the feelings of hurt and betrayal. Let him brainstorm ideas. Write everything down even if it may sound ridiculous. He might suggest he could let it all out and have a good cry, he could tell his friends how he felt, he could repeat an affirmation such as "I value myself," or "I am a good soccer player," he could go outside and kick the soccer ball for a while and so on. You then go through each one with him and look at the pros and cons of each. Your child then chooses the one with more pros and goes and does it.

That is coaching your child through his emotions and how to deal with them.

ACTIVITIES FOR EMOTIONAL DEVELOPMENT

<u>For Attachment</u>

1. Give your baby a massage. After you've finished giving your baby a bath, dry her and place her in the middle of your bed. Make sure there are no drafts. Oil your hands with a gentle oil like pure coconut oil, shea butter or almond oil. Gently stroke your baby's feet, then legs then tummy. Go over her shoulders then down the arms and then the hands. Go slowly and gently. Be aware of what your baby likes and dislikes. Maybe she likes to be stroked on the tummy and not the arms and legs.

2. Play finger rhymes. Hold your baby's hand and say, "Round and round the Kabah like a *hajji*," while using your index finger to draw circles on her palm. Continue with, "One step, two steps..." while walking your fingers up her arm. Then say, "...tickle you under there," and with your walking fingers, gently tickle her under her armpit.

After you play this a few times, your child will begin to anticipate the tickling action and will laugh in delight every time.

<u>To Teach Empathy</u>

1. Use flashcards or photographs of emotions to teach specific emotions.

2. Play pretend. When your child is playing pretend with his stuffed animals, you can guide his play by introducing empathic situations where appropriate. Maybe you can introduce a toy that is lying nearby and say, "Kitty looks so lonely sitting by herself. What can we do to make her feel happy?"

3. Read books that talk about feelings and have a discussion about how the character is feeling.

4. For older children: Spend the day volunteering for a charitable organisation where your child will get to help the poor, lonely or sick, such as a soup kitchen, retirement home or hospital.

Chapter Seven
Cultivating Morality
Hannah Morris

Morality refers to the judgement of right and wrong, and consequent behaviour based on this. Thoughts and behaviours relating to morality change with age in line with other areas of development such as physical, cognitive, emotional and social which have an influence on moral development. Other factors such as the environment in which the child is raised, parenting styles, culture, and society, amongst others, also impact on moral development.

To find out what has the greatest influence on moral development — is it nature or nurture? parents or society? — and whether all children go through the same stages in their moral development, we will look at the theories of moral development.

THEORIES OF MORAL DEVELOPMENT

Piaget (1932)

Piaget was one of the first people to develop a theory of moral development. Belonging to the field of behavioural psychology, his theory was centred on social learning theory and based in line with his theory of cognitive development. Piaget theorised that there are two stages of moral development, each encompassing different motivations of moral reasoning.

1. Heteronomous morality (ages 5-9)

At this stage morality is a result of outside influences, such as parents and educators. Children believe that following rules is the right thing to do and breaking them should result in punishment, and their primary responsibility is telling the truth to adults. At this stage, little or no consideration is afforded to intentions.

2. Autonomous Morality (age 9+)

As they get older, children become influenced by people other than those in authority, namely their peers. Loyalty then belongs to their peers more so than those in authority. For example, a child who sees their friend doing wrong at school will tell the teacher at the heteronomous stage. However, once a child progresses to the autonomous stage, their loyalty switches to that of their peers and they are, therefore, less likely to tell on their friends even if they do something wrong.

They also understand that rules can be changed depending on the circumstances. For example, when running a race with younger children, they are willing to offer them a three second head start in order to be more fair.

As children at this stage consider both intentions and consequences, they may no longer judge an action as wrong if the intentions were good, therefore, reducing the level of blame and consequent level of punishment. For example, a child who stole a bread roll because no one was looking is more blame worthy and deserves a more severe punishment than the one who stole the bread roll to give to the homeless man around the corner who was hungry. Even though the consequences were the same (a bread roll got stolen) the intentions were worse in the first case. Or, someone who lies that they like the jumper that granny knitted him as a gift. They might think that they are not necessarily being immoral by telling a lie as they lied in order to preserve granny's feelings and not undermine her abilities at knitting.

Age	Stage	Description
5-9 years	Heteronomous morality	• Morality is a result of outside influences in authority, e.g. parents. • No consideration of intentions.
9+ years	Autonomous morality	• Morality becomes influenced by those not in authority, e.g. peers. • Intentions are considered.

Table 4.1 Piaget Moral Development

Kohlberg (1958)

Piaget's theory was further developed by Kohlberg, essentially identifying the same route to moral development, with a shift from the initial focus on the influences of those in authority, to considering alternative perspectives in moral decision making in later stages. He proposed three stages of development, each with two levels.

Stage 1: Pre-conventional Morality (Infancy and Preschool Years)

At this stage, children don't yet have their own personal code of morality, instead relying on the opinions of adults in their life and the consequences they assign. Authority outside the individual and reasoning is based on physical consequences of the action. This stage is divided into two levels:

1. **Obedience orientation.** The focus at this stage is that punishment is seen as a means to prevent people doing things that are wrong again. For example, we follow law because we don't want to go to jail.
2. **Instrumental relativist.** Children now understand that there is more than one opinion and the morality of an action is judged on needs of an individual. For example, stealing food because they need it to feed the hungry homeless is seen as acceptable.

Stage 2: Conventional Morality (School Age)

A child now begins to internalise moral viewpoints of adults that they admire and reasoning is based on rules of groups to which they belong. The two levels in this stage are:

1. **Good boy-nice girl orientation.** The morality of an action is judged on societal norms, roles and expectations. For example, a child gives food to the poor because it is seen as a nice thing to do. Children are primarily concerned with the desire to be liked and approved by others.
2. **Law and order orientation.** The focus shifts to respecting authorities, following rules and doing one's duty as they find their place and role in society. For example, they understand that speeding is illegal because of the potential consequences; people can get hurt, the added burden on health care services as a result, and the impact on insurance claims. Having speed limits is therefore understood at a deeper level and they understand the need to follow these rules.

Stage 3: Post-conventional Morality (Teenage Years+)
They have now developed their own sense of morality. This stage is again divided into two levels:

1. **Social contract orientation.** Consideration is given to the opinions of others before forming an opinion of morality. It is understood that laws are mostly good, but sometimes it works against them. For example, speeding is illegal for good reasons, but if they are running late for work, even if the road is clear, they must obey the limit.
2. **Universal ethic principal orientation.** A child or person has developed their own sense of justice.

Age	Stage		Description
Infancy and preschool	Preconventional morality No individual code of morality yet	1. Obedience orientation	Punishment stops people doing bad things.
		2. Instrumental relativist	Understands there is more than one opinion to be considered.
School Age	Conventional morality Begin to internalise moral	1. Good boy-nice girl orientation	Morality is judged by social norms.
		2. Law and order	Focus on doing one's role in

		viewpoints	orientation	society and respecting societal rules.
Teenage +		Post-conventional morality	1. Social contract orientation	Considers the opinions of others.
		Own sense of morality is developed	2. Universal ethic principal orientation	Developes their own sense of justice.

Table 4.2 Kohlberg Moral Development

Whilst many people have criticised these theories due to issues of bias and sample used to generate these theories, findings have been successfully replicated and can be useful in guiding parents and educators.

FACTORS THAT INFLUENCE MORAL DEVELOPMENT NEGATIVELY

Most aspects of child development are influenced by both innate factors, caused by genetics, and external factors, caused by environment and social influences, however, morality is influenced more through external factors. This can be positive, although, there are instances where the impact on the child's moral development can be problematic that parents should be aware of to avoid negative consequences.

Parental Styles

Democratic parenting is much more likely to promote the development of internal self-controls and moral growth. Permissive parents however, do not show any control over their children, and authoritarian parenting creates fear of punishment.

Bad Role Models

We know that children look to those in authority as their moral decision makers, especially during the earlier stages of moral development, therefore an authority figure who makes bad moral decisions will encourage the child to do so too.

Contempt and Humiliation

This leads to a misunderstanding of reward and punishment.

Family Problems

Confrontation between parents, especially in front of the child, can cause a sense of insecurity for the child as well as confusion over good moral behaviour. This leaves a gateway for the child to commit immoral behaviour as a result of their internal feelings.

Spoiling Children

Much like children of permissive parents, children who are spoilt develop distorted moral perceptions as they are seldom given the opportunity to take responsibility. Therefore, they can become arrogant, and rebel and disrespect authority as the roles are almost reversed because the authority figure is controlled by the child.

Non-religious Society

Each society or culture has its own set of norms. For example, in Islam sex before marriage, extramarital affairs and homosexuality are immoral, yet it is accepted in the West and there are even laws to protect them. In fact, it is seen as immoral to discriminate against homosexuals in some countries. This can be particularly difficult for Muslim children raised in Western countries as they face a conflict between what is morally right and wrong between their cultural upbringing and that of the society in which they live.

Trauma

Abuse and witnessing abuse causes children to challenge and see the world as unjust and unfair.

COMMON PARENTAL CONCERNS

Rebellion may be encountered as the child reaches the stage where they realise that other people may have different moral opinions to those in authority whom they previously obeyed. As they develop their own belief system and find and establish their place in world, they usually become less rebellious.

Most children behave immorally at times and this is all part of the process of moral development. Once a child enters the stage where they become aware of the moral views of peers, they can become vulnerable to peer pressures into more risky and immoral behaviours, such as alcohol and drugs. However, when lack of self confidence and defiance become issues that are having a severe effect on their wellbeing and those around them, this may be part of a psychological disorder that requires further intervention.

It is particularly concerning if the child shows a lack of acceptance or remorse after having committed violent or destructive behaviour and may be an indication of a more serious psychological disorder.

WHAT IS THE ISLAMIC PERSPECTIVE ON MORAL DEVELOPMENT AND MORALITY?

As an entire way of life, Islam has much to teach us about morality as it is one of the most important aspects of character development. We can use this information to successfully teach and guide children in their moral development. There are numerous examples in the Quran and Sunnah that guide us on what morality is and how to achieve it both individually and as a society.

The Islamic way of life teaches how to deal with issues relating to morality and the importance of being of good moral character.

"The best of you is the best among you in conduct." (Al-Bukhari 3559)

It is expected that people not only exhibit such traits themselves, but encourage this in others also, especially our children who are learning.

"You are the best nation produced [as an example] for mankind. You enjoin what is right and forbid what is wrong and believe in Allah. If only the People of the Scripture had believed, it would have been better for them. Among them are believers, but most of them are defiantly disobedient." (Quran 3:110)

Morality in terms of the character of a Muslim is very simply defined in the Quran.

"Righteousness is not that you turn your faces toward the east or the west, but [true] righteousness is [in] one who believes in Allah, the Last Day, the angels, the Book, and the prophets and gives wealth, in spite of love for it, to relatives, orphans, the needy, the traveller, those who ask [for help], and for freeing slaves; [and who] establishes prayer and gives zakah; [those who] fulfill their promise when they promise; and [those who] are patient in poverty and hardship and during battle. Those are the ones who have been true, and it is those who are the righteous." (Quran 2:177)

This verse teaches us that the key to good conduct and morality lies in a strong relation with Allah ﷻ who knows the intentions behind all actions. Therefore, when we keep Allah ﷻ in mind at all times and in all intentions, we will behave with the best moral character.

There are many moral teachings in Islam for various aspects of a Muslim's life. They cover the broad spectrum of personal moral conduct of a Muslim as well as their social responsibilities, including, being of good character, treatment of others, and manners in certain situations.

Being of Good Character

Good manners and abstaining from using bad language

Abud-Darda ﷺ reported, "The Prophet ﷺ said, 'Nothing will be heavier on the Day of Resurrection in the Scale of the believer than good manners. Allah hates one who utters foul or coarse language.'" (At-Tirmidhi, 626)

Good Treatment of Others

Parents

"And your Lord has decreed that you not worship except Him, and to parents, good treatment. Whether one or both of them reach old age [while] with you, say not to them [so much as], "uff," and do not repel them but speak to them a noble word." (Quran 17:23)

Other Relatives

"And give the relative his right, and [also] the poor and the traveller, and do not spend wastefully." (Quran 17:26)

Neighbours

Ibn 'Abbas told Ibn az-Zubayr, "I heard the Prophet ﷺ say, 'A man is not a believer who fills his stomach while his neighbour is hungry.'" (Al-Adab Al-Mufrad 112)

Manners in Certain Situations

Visiting Others

"O you who have believed, do not enter houses other than your own houses until you ascertain welcome and greet their inhabitants. That is best for you; perhaps you will be reminded." (Quran 24:27)

In a Gathering

"O you who have believed, when you are told, "Space yourselves" in assemblies, then make space; Allah will make space for you. And when you are told, "Arise," then arise; Allah will raise those who have believed among you and those who were given knowledge, by degrees. And Allah is Acquainted with what you do." (Quran 58:11)

These moral behaviours are not only important to the individual, but to the society as a whole.

How Can a Parent or Educator Instil Morality and Support Moral Development from an Islamic Perspective?

Implementation of these things encourage good moral conduct which in turn is best for mankind as a whole. It helps to purify the souls against things such as selfishness, egotism, and oppression, instead fostering an Allah ﷻ conscious, disciplined approach to life, full of kindness and compassion, fairness and truthfulness in all situations.

But, how do we instil these morals in our children? Imam Al-Ghazalli offers excellent advice to answer this question.

"Religious morals will not be instilled in the soul except when the person gets used to all good habits, leaves all bad acts, regularly practices and enjoys doing good acts, and hates and feels pain concerning bad acts. Good morals are acquired by getting accustomed to good acts and watching and accompanying those who do good acts – those people are the companions of goodness and the brothers of righteousness.

Dispositions copy from each other, and good and evil are equal in this respect. Children are, in principle, disciplined by keeping them away from evil friends. Every human being is born with a sound innate disposition, and his morals are refined by regular observation and upbringing. The boy should be honoured and rewarded with something that he loves and be praised in front of people whenever he shows good manners and does a commendable act. If he violates the proper conduct once, he should be overlooked; if he repeats it, he should be blamed secretly without over-reprimanding him every now and then. This actually makes blame insignificant in his heart. It is preferable that the father maintains his solemnity above blaming him, whereas the mother intimidates him by the father."

Essentially, what is being referred to here can be likened to the previous stages of moral development, especially during the early stages where reward and punishment are relied upon to promote healthy moral development. This process of reward and punishment in the early stages helps to mold a child with good moral characteristics in line with Islamic teachings. This is the easiest way to reinforce the difference between right and wrong in a child. It is the responsibility of the parents and educators to nurture these characteristics.

These are things we can take from Islam. For example, Allah ﷻ doesn't punish unjustly, so neither should we. If they hurt themselves we do not have to add pain to injury, similarly, there will be times where we are punished for a sin in this life and not again for the same sin in the Hereafter. Also, just as Allah ﷻ rewards and punishes by intention, children should be punished by their intention. Therefore, if they conduct an act of moral misconduct by mistake, or by accident, then they need not be punished harshly. We can use these teachings to use punishment most effectively as a means to nurture moral development. Being a good role model and delivering punishments fairly and respectfully will also be part of assisting their moral development.

TIPS AND ACTIVITIES TO CULTIVATE MORALITY

Moral development begins from an early age as we know from the stages of moral development. There are many ways in which you can ensure a good moral upbringing and teach lessons of morality naturally in daily life, as well as specific activities that can be done with your child to teach moral development.

Being a positive role model is the first step in encouraging positive moral development, especially in the early years when authority figures provide the source of education through actions of what is right or wrong. For example, be fair when resolving arguments and keep your promises.

Praise and positive discipline is achieved by reinforcing and praising good choices, as well as highlighting bad choices by emphasising that it was not the best choice and why, especially after the first time that these behaviours have been carried out. Praise good moral behavior, such as sharing and being kind, and encouraging such behaviours daily will encourage them to repeat good acts again.

It is important that your child receive fair punishment for any moral wrongdoings to assist them in identifying the link between their behaviour and the consequences. For example, if your child is not punished or redirected in some way for doing an immoral act, such as stealing, then they will learn that it is ok to steal.

Discuss how their behaviour affects others, for example, ask your child how stealing will make the one you stole from upset. This helps your child to consider consequences of their actions both in terms of punishment for bad behaviour, but also consider the consequences for others too. On top of this, encourage them to consider natural consequences for their actions too. For example, if your child continually lies, then no one will trust them anymore.

Discuss hypothetical situations where your child can think about all options and their consequences. For example, asking what they would do if they saw their friend stealing.

It is important to set and discuss reasons for rules and why certain behaviours are better than others. For example, sharing toys is better than telling other children to go away as it will make the other child happy too. Telling them to go away might upset them. This teaches moral reasoning, empathy, and perspective taking; skills that promote positive moral decision making. This is particularly important during the early years when following rules is the only aspect of moral reasoning that is understood as your child is motivated to follow rules to avoid punishment. It is therefore important that it is made clear to them what the rules are, why they are important, and the consequences should they be broken.

Activities

Telling and Reading Stories

There are many moral story books available that teach morals, such as 'The Boy who cried wolf'. To extend this further, you can encourage your child to pick a moral and write their own story on the topic.

Caring for a Plant or a Pet

Taking care of things other than humans can also give your child the opportunity to think of the needs of others and develop a sense of empathy that will promote alternative perspective taking. This will encourage your child to think beyond themselves when engaging in moral decision making. Developing such skills towards non-human objects is a means to practice the skills they use with fellow humans behaving in a more kind and compassionate way.

Classification Game

In this game, draw two columns on a piece of paper; one for good deeds and one for bad deeds. Your child can either design a set of cards with good and bad deeds on them to cut out and sort onto the chart, or they can draw them straight into the chart. As they put a deed in each column, they should be encouraged to explain why they are putting it in the selected column.

Moral of the Day

Pick one moral from a hadith or Quranic ayat, such as kindness or patience, as the moral for the day or week and discuss ways to implement it. Every time your child exhibits this trait they are rewarded with a gold star on a star chart.

A Moral Role Model Project

We know that children learn right and wrong from those in authority so you can ask your child to pick a historical role model in Islamic history, such as a Prophet or a Sahaba. They can conduct a research project on this character, presenting all their positive moral traits and present an oral or written report.

These are just some ideas to get you started on cultivating your child's moral character.

ABOUT THE AUTHORS

Chapter 1: Developing Thinking Skills

Chapter 6: Fostering Emotional Development

Jameela Ho is a mother and teacher. She is also a PhD candidate researching cognition and learning. She holds a Diploma of Counselling and blogs on the subject of both education and parenting on two separate blogs.

ILMA Education (**www.ilmaeducation**) is where she helps parents nurture their children's growing mind. Her other blog is Muslim Parenting (**www.jameelaho.com**) where she helps parents raise their children with the love of Islam.

Chapter 2: Facilitating Intelligence

Irna Fathurrubayah is a teacher, writer and blogger. She holds a Bachelor Degree in Mathematics Education where she started her career as an assistant teacher in an Elementary School which for her was the most meaningful experience in understanding children. She currently works as an elementary school teacher. Her interests are in the area of Brain science, Psychology and Digital Citizenship.

Besides teaching, she has just started her journey as a freelance writer and author. In her spare time she writes on her personal blog **https://rubayahnote.wordpress.com/** and she is currently working on her Educational website Atfalna Education which will be launched soon.

Chapter 3: Supporting Speech & Language Development

Weronika trained as a Speech and Language Therapist at De Montfort University and then went on to do postgraduate research in autism and bilingualism at the University of Reading. Now she lives in the South West of England with her husband and homeschools their four young children.

Weronika shares information about her multicultural family life on her blog, **Multicultural Motherhood**, as well as her **YouTube channel** where she shares information about homeschooling, bilingualism and speech and language issues. She can also be found on social media.

Chapter 4: Promoting Motor Skills

Nabila Ikram obtained her B.A. in Education from the University of Michigan-Dearborn. She has worked in a number of educational settings, including the classroom and youth mentorship programs, and has conducted and presented research in multiculturalism and literacy.

After starting a family, Nabila's professional interests took on a more personal feel as she observed her own children's learning and development. Desiring to stay home with her children, she decided to focus her energy on developing **Everlearning Everlasting** with a stronger focus on learning as a natural lifelong journey and the importance of family wellness as a mainstay of a rich and valuable education.

Chapter 5: Nurturing Healthy Physical Growth

Afshan Mohammed is 28 years old and lives in Houston, TX. She completed her undergraduate degree in Nutrition at University of Houston and then her Dietetic Internship, her Master's degree in Nutrition at Texas Woman's University. She worked at Texas Children's Hospital for 4 years with children who have diabetes, until she recently had her baby daughter.

Her hobbies include volunteering, reading, taking long walks at the park, and traveling. She takes Islamic Courses in Houston with Sameera Institute.

Chapter 7: Cultivating Morality

Hannah Morris is a mum of 5 aged between 5 months and 11 years.

She is originally from the UK but currently residing in the Republic of Ireland. She holds Master's degrees in both Psychological Science and Health Psychology. She has spent many years working in psychiatric hospitals and in residential care facilities for children and adolescence with emotional and behavioural difficulties. She is presently working as a lecturer in Psychology with the Islamic Online University.

Hannah has a passion for writing children's books and is currently working on a series of books that aim to teach children skills such as mindfulness and stress management to nurture their psychological wellbeing through storytelling and supporting activities. She can be found at **www.the5bankieteers.com** where she presents information relating to these books and provides support for parents to learn the skills to work with their children in nurturing the skills taught in the books.

www.ingramcontent.com/pod-product-compliance
Lightning Source LLC
Chambersburg PA
CBHW070521100426
42743CB00010B/1901